I 'spect I grow'd

A Cotswold childhood and teenage years during the 1930s and 1940s

Derrick Whitehouse

authorHOUSE®

AuthorHouse™ UK Ltd.
500 Avebury Boulevard
Central Milton Keynes, MK9 2BE
www.authorhouse.co.uk
Phone: 08001974150

© 2010 Derrick Whitehouse. All rights reserved.

No part of this book may be reproduced, stored in a retrieval system, or transmitted by any means without the written permission of the author. First published by AuthorHouse

ISBN: 978-1-4490-9041-8 (sc)

Contents

Preface — vii

Foreword — ix

Acknowledgements — xi

Chapter One: The pre-school years from 1932 to 1937 — 1

Chapter two: The Infant school years from 1937 to 1940 — 19

Chapter three: The Junior school years
– aged seven to eleven from 1940 to 1944 — 27

Chapter four: The Secondary School years
from 1944 to 1950 — 53

More photographs of Chipping Campden Grammar School — 77

More photographs of Moreton Scout Troop in the 1940s — 78

Chapter five: The post-school years from 1950 to 1955 — 81

Epilogue : As Time Goes By! The continuing story of
nostalgia and questing into the 21st century — 91

Preface

This is a book which takes me back through the eyes and experience of a child and teenager but with the hindsight that is overlaid by the knowledge and experience of an adult.

The writing of this story has come about after realising that there is no extensive record of life in Moreton and district that I am aware of during the 1930s and 1940s as seen through the eyes and experience of a boy growing up during those momentous years. During the years of the Second World War many people were away from the area and were in no position to observe the antics and development of the local children and teenagers, which may include some of the mischief we got up to. It would seem that even those who were around have been understandably reluctant to put pen to paper.

Looking back on my early life I have come to realise that in so many ways I lived during an idyllic yet turbulent period for growing up and as one gets older these significant and influential events come flooding back.

In presenting this account it is an attempt at unfolding something of the social history of the time in the Moreton area. It is a very personal account and I have made no concessions in holding back on some of the incidents in my life and the life of those living in Moreton and the surrounding environs. This is all done to produce a flavour of the life a working class lad led, warts and all. I am not fearful of being embarrassed but where names of others are mentioned I shall try hard not to humiliate them or their relatives in any way. Many of those I grew up with are still around and this book is dedicated to them as well as those who are no longer with us. I have been known to wander round the cemetery looking at names on tombstones and recalling what each person contributed to local life. However, it is hoped that this modest volume will appeal to newcomers in the area many of whom will have had similar experiences of growing up elsewhere during the 1930s and 1940s.

Although over the years I have lived and worked in many parts of Britain there has always been a compulsion to visit Moreton over and over again. Every time I do this I have to go on a tour of inspection to look at the changes as well as recall how things were in earlier times. These are the times recorded here, which I hope will give an air of nostalgia for the locals and present newcomers with a historical perspective on this beautiful and vibrant part of the country.

As a member of the Religious Society of Friends (Quakers) I visit regularly and worship with the members of the Local Meeting at Broad Campden in their historic Meeting House.

I owe much to my parents and maternal grandparents and many others who will come alive in the subsequent text, for presenting me with the opportunity to grow up and be nurtured in this picturesque and wonderful part of Britain known as the Cotswolds. Also I dedicate this work to my wife of over fifty years and to my children and grandchildren who all love the location as much as I do.

May those who read this get pleasure from the rendition of my experience as much as I have enjoyed recalling and writing about my early days of growing up in Moreton-in-Marsh and its environs.

Derrick R. Whitehouse

Foreword

The place where you were born and grew up never leaves you no matter how far away you roam. The memories are always with you of the things that helped shape you long ago when you were young. Derrick Whitehouse was fortunate in his place of birth, a small Cotswold town with a broad main street-cum-market place lined with mellow houses and tall trees. Moreton-in-Marsh by name. As a close-knit country community it gave him from the outset a very real sense of belonging. When he was there it had a population of about 1,900: big enough to justify its status as a town, with shops, hospital and hotels, yet small enough for its people to know each other by sight if not by name. A quiet friendly place it was an apt environment for someone eventually to become a significant figure in the Quaker movement.

The Second World War preoccupied his early years and gave an added spice of adventure. He always seems to have had a fascination with uniform and saw it in abundance with the local Home Guard, the advent of British troops, then the Yanks who treated him as some kind of mascot, and then the RAF which had a hastily built operational air base nearby. In the immediate post-war years he himself became uniformed by joining the Scouts and Air Cadets. It had always been his dream to become an airman, which came true with conscription opening up service with the RAF at home and in the Far East on multifarious duties.

I first got to know him when I came to Moreton in January 1948 as a journalist for a local newspaper. While I stayed he left home for many years to seek a career but we have always kept in touch since then. I've marvelled at his going to college to train as a teacher after leaving the RAF, then going after further major educational and social qualifications culminating in a doctorate. He has achieved much but could not have done so without the encouragement and support of his talented wife, Ruth, and support of his children, three boys and a girl. He has now added to his laurels with this remarkable publication about growing up in his native town, which he has never forgotten. And with this book Moreton-in-Marsh will not forget him either.

David B. Day

DAVID DAY has lived in Moreton-in-Marsh for 60 years and at various times has been a journalist, founder member of the Local History Society, chairman of the Town hall Committee, clerk to Bourton-on-the-Hill Parish Council and tourist information officer. He has written three books, *The Bevin Boy (1975), All Over The Wold (1998) and The Duck Pond Affair Etc. (2005).* He also wrote a history of the 60-year old Moreton Agricultural and Horse Show.

Acknowledgements

When producing any book it inevitably turns into a team effort and this volume is no exception. I am so grateful for the help and support that has been provided by a number of people some of whom have been inspirational. This particular quest started with a conversation one Sunday afternoon at the Wellington Museum at Moreton-in-Marsh with Gerald Tyack the owner. For nearly two hours we found ourselves reminiscing over the years of the Second World War. It was soon realised by both of us that there were stories and anecdotes that neither of us had heard. When I got home I came to the conclusion that the stories needed to be told. Consequently, I have been regularly encouraged by Gerald who has also allowed me to use a number of photographs from his extensive collection.

As the writing progressed Guy Stapleton has been helpful and supportive and has also supplied me with a good number of photographs from the Reg Drury collection of which he is the main custodian as well as from his own sources. Guy has also been a great help in promoting the book through the local History Societies at Moreton and Chipping Campden.

My long-standing and much loved friend from the 1940s David Day has been a considerable help and well-wisher. He read an early draft, which he corrected in places as well as suggesting some improvements to the text. He also agreed to provide the Foreword, which with our long friendship makes him the most appropriate person for the task.

Others have also contributed. My wife amongst her many virtues is also an excellent proof reader. Consequently, over the whole gestation period of the production she has been available to check and make comments. In addition my family, who are all discerning readers, have made their views on the composition well known.

Making the photographs presentable has been a major task as many of them were originally taken with a Brownie Box camera (the only device available during the times under review). Therefore, I am grateful for the help provide by a friend Ian Draper for work on improving some pictures as well as allowing the use of a photograph of the Town Hall for the front cover taken by his father during the pre-WW2 period when on a day trip from Birmingham. I am also thankful for the services of AuthorHouse Publishing which has provided an excellent package for self publishing so that the book will appear both presentable and acceptable to the readers.

Finally to the memory of those individuals in the Moreton and Campden area who were my friends and associates and whose involvement in my life made this production a reality and possible as a social document illustrating the life and times in the North Cotswolds during the 1930s and 1940s.

Chapter One

The pre-school years from 1932 to 1937

This adventure started on the 22nd November 1932 at the Moreton-in-Marsh Cottage Hospital. I was to be the one and only child of Alfred Robert Whitehouse (known as Bob) and his wife Evelyn May.

My father had moved to Moreton from London in the late 1920s to work as a driver for Percy Sheen, known to everyone as Squeaker due to his high-pitched voice. Percy loved horses, owned a hardware shop and a bus. The shop is now owned by Ben Jeffrey, an immigrant from Draycott with whom I was at school. Initially my father drove Mr. Sheen's bus, which included taking the young people to Chipping Campden Grammar School. He also taught one or two of the locals to drive, which included Jack Bull and Percy Lloyd.

Bob Whitehouse (standing) and Jack Bull (in Bus) drivers of Percy Sheen's bus around 1931.

Derrick Whitehouse

After a while he decided to branch out on his own with a taxi. His first car was an American Hudson Essex

My mother was the youngest daughter of Ernest and Priscilla Prew who lived at Campden Ash a farmstead on the Springhill Estate owned by Captain Hannay. There were three sons, Maxwell, Robert and Lennox. The latter still lives at Spring Hill. Before marriage the Hannay family had employed my mother, educated at Blockley Girls School, as a Nursery maid where, fortunately for me, she learned a good deal about bringing up children.

Our first home as a family was in the rather portentous building on the High Street, next to what is now the District Council Offices and known today as Compton House. My father's taxi was housed in the extensive garage and car repair facility next door owned by a Mr. Jack Crowhurst (now the small shopping precinct – photograph below was taken around the outbreak of WW2, which includes his later vehicle a Hudson

Terraplane, which was drooled over by all the local lads as such a streamlined American car had not been seen in the area till then). A Mr Parker known as Nossy, presumably a corruption of nosy, owned the house. He had a grocery shop and café in the building later known as the 'Kettle Boils' and now called 'Tilley's'.

Photo by the Gloucestershire Echo

We lived in that house until around 1940 when we had to move due to what I now understand to have probably been a compulsory purchase to provide further space for offices with the Rural District Council at the outbreak of the Second World War. It became the Food Office and housed other essential administrative needs. The garage next door was commandeered to be turned into a Decontamination Centre (fortunately never needed).

Living where we did provided me with, even as a young child, a vantage point to observe what was going on in Moreton High Street. Remember that this was the 1930s so life then was not as frenetic as it is today. Quite often during the day the street was at a standstill especially as all the shops closed for lunch as well as Wednesday being early closing day.

Mornings were always fairly busy with people doing their shopping. Folks arrived either on foot or on bicycles. There was also a smattering of ramshackle cars and vans plus several horse drawn carts from the outlying area.

A major event for this small boy each day was to watch the milkman delivering. Our man was Charlie Currill and the milk cart was classic horse drawn, painted cream and brown, with a brass churn. Charlie would come along with a bucket of milk plus measures for a pint and half pint and would ladle out a pint or two into waiting jugs. He worked for Mr. Tarplett the owner of the dairy farm (the milking sheds and his home were on the corner of Church Street, opposite what is now the Manor House Hotel). The cows grazed in the fields at the end of the road past the horse pond, although sometimes they were in the Dorn fields, which meant the herd was driven back and forth by Billy Tarplett on his bicycle, the length of the High Street.

At my very young age I had two favourite shops. First, was Hooper's (now where the dining room of the Black Bear is situated) for newspapers, and sweets. I would often be given either a penny or halfpenny to go along and buy a bar of chocolate. Second was the toy shop owned by Oliver and Mrs Emes (now owned by the Cotswold Bookstore). Oliver cut men's hair and his wife managed the toys – Dinky toys were my favourite and I, a lucky boy, had quite a few over the years of childhood.

I 'spect I grow'd

Mr Parker's shop Mrs Emes

My first haircut was with Mr Talbot who had his parlour and family home in what was then referred to as the Old Post Office, which is next door to the Bell Inn. I recall that this was quite a traumatic experience but I got over it. However, I do remember that Mr Talbot had around him his daughters, one of whom was Molly who in later years became a Moreton 'character' under her married name of Molly Jelly – I seem to remember that Molly used to take me for walks in my pram. Her brother in those days just at the point of leaving school was Barry who later became the proprietor of Barry's coaches.

Tuesday was market day, but nothing like the present day with the High Street clogged by stalls and people. There were three, possibly four or five, market areas mainly for the farming community. The pig market was located in the area behind the Redesdale Arms Hotel in Hospital Road. The sheep, cattle and poultry market was to be found where the car park is now sited. On the opposite side of the road adjacent to the Scout HQ was the covered Produce Market for eggs, butter and cheese, now part of Coachman's Court. The great attraction for youngsters was that the facilities for cows, sheep and pigs provided what today would be termed an Adventure Playground. There was a raised platform, for the auctioneer, running the length of the sheep and pigpens as well as loads of railings to climb up and over. All was well until the caretaker came and chased us off the premises.

Market day was full of excitement for me as a small boy looking out of the window on to the gravelled and potholed High Street. There was always something interesting going on especially at closing times for the public houses. The Black Bear was where many congregated especially the gypsy fraternity and I often watched as the local police were called out to march away one or two who had had a drink too many. Two local characters who were often visible on market day were Tilly Hardiman, an eccentric woman with a large brimmed hat who liked her tipple and then there was a similar character known to everyone as Mrs 'Bladder' Brown. It seems people enjoy using alliteration to describe personalities.

During the fine weather, especially at weekends before the War started, the town was always busy during the day with hoards of cyclists from the Midlands out for a 'spin'. These were in the main cycling clubs and they arrived in groups of anything up to fifty or more. There were always several groups coming and going. Some would stop in Moreton for refreshment whilst others were passing through and onwards to other Cotswold beauty spots.

There were also from time to time others who strutted up and down the main street and were travelling street entertainers. I vividly remember two men with fiddles dressed in top hat and tails who often came to parade up and down whilst playing for the public. I loved them in their splendour and it was a major highlight of my childlike viewing. Other occasional visitors included a scissor grinder complete with his contraption, which he pushed around then sat and paddled the grinding wheels

I 'spect I grow'd

to sharpen not just scissors but any implements with a blade. In addition a welcome visitor was the Wall's *Stop me and Buy one* tricycle that toured the villages to sell delicious ice cream and iced lollies. From time to time on a Saturday morning Billy Timms a farmer from Dorn would come in with his horse and cart loaded with produce to sell. Sitting quietly on the cart were his son and daughter Catherine and young Billy who later became great friends of mine and Catherine emerging as a well-known Moreton personality.

Another highlight was during the winter months around four o'clock in the afternoon when little Jimmy Radburn (he was short with a hump on his back), the Lamplighter would arrive with his ladder and systematically move along the High Street igniting all the gas lamps, the only illumination we had in those days. I cannot help but to recall a popular song of the time *The Old Lamplighter – He made the night a little brighter beneath the candle glow, that old lamplighter of long long ago.* In fact most houses still had gas lamps and cookers. It was in the late thirties that the Shropshire, Worcester and Staffordshire Electricity Board installed electricity to our home. The local HQ of this company was in the Square at Stow-on-the-Wold.

Derrick Whitehouse

A fairly regular and very exciting happening was to watch the local Merryweather motor fire engine with crew speeding up the High Street either on an exercise or actually going to put out a fire, possibly a hayrick being the usual problem. The wonderful thing about this spectacle was that the machine was one of the old red engines with an ornate ladder running the length. However the most spectacular part was that the firemen would be standing on a running board either side wearing their tall highly polished pointed brass fire helmets. They were magnificent and the fire chief was I believe Bert Clayton the local blacksmith and the driver Fred Weller who was also the driver of the Rural District Council dustcart. The fire station was the building on the corner of East Street and still there for another purpose. When the Second World War arrived the beautiful fire engine was scrapped and a green van pulling a fire unit was the replacement, not anything like so impressive although probably more efficient.

In our home there were other diversions. Around that time the Council Offices were being created in the building with similar frontage to the present day, which had been the home and drapers' shop of the Sankey family. The son John Sankey was given a peerage and became Viscount John Sankey of Moreton-in-Marsh (father Thomas, mother Catalina), rising to be Lord Chancellor 1929 to 1935: born 1866 died 1948. He was buried in Moreton Cemetery on 10th February 1948 aged 82 years. I remember my father telling me that a well-known local man called Ray Beddows, who helped in the adjacent garage and small print shop, had played as a small boy with John Sankey.

For a while we had living with us on the top floor of the building Alec and Ethel Baldwin. Alec was the foreman for the development of the RDC building, later moving with daughter Barbara to Number one Redesdale Place, which was being built at around that same time just before WW2.

At a similar time one of the ground-floor rooms of our house was given over to the office of the Evesham Journal & Four Shires Advertiser. We had two incumbents, first Mr Sisam then Geoffrey Carver, as the local reporters. When they were both called away to the War my mother stepped in to collect any advertising that was brought in and the full office was disbanded. We also offered hospitality for lunch to Bill White who was a local policeman. (I found him a bit scary – actually he was a very nice chap and later married one of the daughters of the Thomas family who owned the Cotswold Cafe).

When living in Moreton one of the great joys is that there are so many places to walk in every direction. However, one wonderful place for walking in the 1930s and much earlier was Moreton Common (or Batsford Heath as it is referred to on some old maps). This is the area occupied formerly by the RAF airfield and now the Fire Service College. I recall the locale having an open network of footpaths and gorse bushes stretching across as far as Wolford Woods. On a spring or summer evening one could find half the population out walking. Sadly I was still too young to enjoy the space as yet another playground before it was commandeered for other purposes. It is worth calling to mind that it was this lovely stretch of land that led to one of the reasons for Moreton having the Curfew Bell and Tower to be a guide at dusk for bringing homewards those who were out on the common in the gloom.

Derrick Whitehouse

Adapted from a painting by Sean Bolan entitled *The Arrival at Moreton-in-Marsh* and reproduced by courtesy of S and V Farnsworth, Grimes Cottage Gallery

One of the favourite things to do as a three and four year old was to go to the railway station with my mother to watch the trains coming and going. We used to go along during the late afternoon when the smaller train based at Moreton was engaged in shunting trucks and containers with milk and dairy produce at the adjacent United Dairy (or the Creamery as the locals referred to it) ready to be attached to the evening train for London. This was exciting for such a small boy and at times in the process the engine would come alongside the platform and I was able to talk to the driver and the fireman who was Ted Hardiman. Ted was always amusing and a great character. Once or twice I was allowed to step on the footplate and what was even more exciting, I rode with them to do part of the shunting operation. Oddly enough I never hankered after becoming a train driver. Once a week this engine would spend the whole day carrying trucks on the branch line to Shipston-on-Stour and possibly stopping at other village stations on the way. It was a slow journey as the lines were not always in the best state of repair as this was the only train in the week. In former years the railway line went right through to Stratford-

I 'spect I grow'd

upon-Avon, where originally the carriages were horse-drawn. Even today when driving towards Stratford it is still possible to discern the route taken.

Another favourite pastime, not just for me but practically for the majority of Moreton children, was to gaze in wonder at the ornamental sculptures and models in stone in the garden created by the Smith family in a garden-like area located opposite the horse pond. Fred Smith was a monumental mason with his workshop behind the garden. As well as admiring the variety of models on show (see photograph) the real attraction for children was the wall that separated the garden from the Stow road footpath. This was quite low, no more than around three feet high, but every six feet or so, there were balls of stone about a foot in diameter. It needs little imagination to visualise every child walking along the wall and either jumping over the balls or standing on each one in turn as we progressed from one end to the other. This whole area was a beautiful feature in the town and much appreciated by everyone.

Derrick Whitehouse

It always seemed to me that the whole population turned out for certain events, the annual Church fete being one, which was held in the garden of the Rectory. Apart from the usual stalls for produce and tests of skill there was also entertainment. I call to mind two groups in particular. There was the Girls' Training Corps (GTC) a quasi-military group for young women run by one of the teachers Megan Jones, at what was then called the senior school. They performed various sketches and the one I now recall was a clash between Tweedledum and Tweedledee. The other group that performed regularly was the dancers from Miss Isitt's School of Dancing. At that time Miss Isitt was a teacher at St David's Church of England Junior School. Later she became the Head of the Dormer House School. At the time all these performances appeared to be quite enchanting to my young mind.

Perhaps The major event of the year was the ox-roast and fair, which was held early in September. The traditional fair is still held around that time but alas the ox-roast tradition has long died out. However, there are still photographs around of this event and I am able to identify most of the people in the depiction. In particular there was the local butcher, Charlie Drury and some of his employees and amongst others there were Sid Mace (who with his father owned a bicycle sales and repair shop) and Mr. Harrison, Headmaster of the Senior School, known as Boss to all his pupils. Naturally the roasting of the ox took a considerable time with the carcass of such a large animal being revolved on a spit and basted, which meant an early morning start in order to prepare the meat for dispensing at the appropriate hour. However, this was all part of the ritual with people standing and watching the cooking process. Then when all was ready folks would come forward with their plates to collect cuts of meat from the roasted animal, some collecting for the whole family. I assume there was some form of payment but I was too young to understand the mechanics of that operation. Above all it was a spectacle for people to get pleasure from with the event being very rustic in concept.

In those days the fair spread the length and breadth of the High Street having all the usual fairground attractions such as the ginny horses, dodgems and the cakewalk, which the latter we no longer have but I remember seeing long queues of people waiting to take the walk with every step taking the feet and body in a different direction. There were also vendors selling their wares usually referred to by the locals as 'cheap jacks'. I recollect being mesmerised as they threw several plates into the air at one time only to catch them into a neat stack. For a small boy this was really something to behold and is still fixed in my memory even as I approach my late seventies.

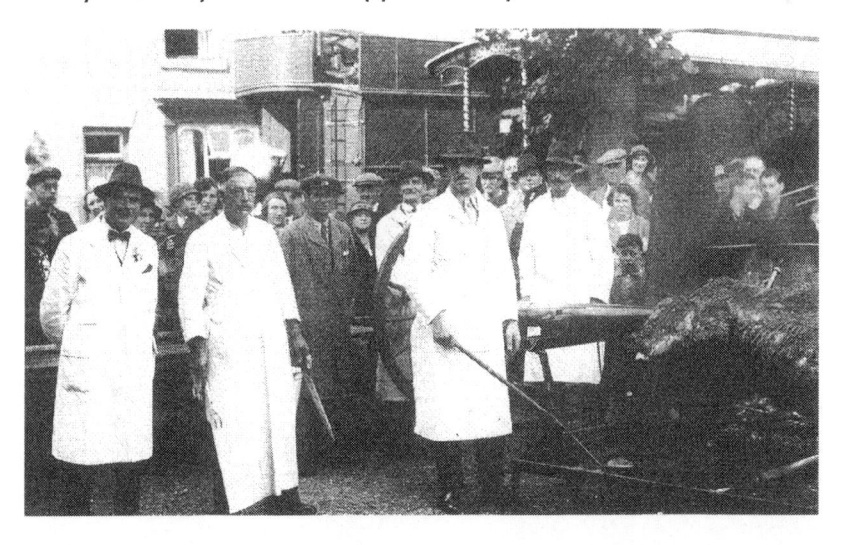

The High Street has not always been as well surfaced as it is today. I recall it having dips in places and rough gravel on top. Consequently with heavy rain there was some flooding (I hasten to say that flooding was nothing like as severe as the experience of more recent years). However the lower end of town around the Manor House Hotel and up to the Swan Hotel was always vulnerable. I am not aware of the flood ever entering premises – but could be wrong. Also there were huge puddles at other points, which presented opportunities to go paddling in our wellies. Fortunately drainage was fairly effective and the problem was never long lasting. Nevertheless it was rather frightening at the time.

As an only child living in the High Street there were very few other children nearby to play with. Consequently, during those pre-school years I was subject to a sheltered existence as far as playmates were concerned. My mother had women friends with young children all of whom were up to eighteen months older than me. Knowing a good deal about child development I now realise there is a noticeable difference in the way children play and develop when even just twelve months apart. As a result as I now look back I realise I continued to be for most of the time an observer of what others were doing. The children I encountered at this time were Barbara Bond (wife of Cecil Tarplett), David Coxhill (more about David in a later chapter) and Peter Lloyd who has been a lifelong friend ever since. (Peter a notable Moreton Footballer, moved to live in Australia but we continued to talk, at considerable length, to each other regularly until his death in September 2009).

The photograph with Barbara Tarplett, who I have known for most of my life, was taken during early teenage years. Barbara, her mother and grandmother were frequent visitors to the home of my grand-parents at Campden Ash on the Springhill Estate

Perhaps my first pre-school encounter with other children en masse was on two distinctive national occasions, namely, the Jubilee Celebration for George V and the Coronation of George VI. For both these events all the local children had parties, which were held in the British Legion in Station Road. For me they were bewildering events where children untamed and full of life were let loose to demolish mountains of fish paste sandwiches followed by jelly and blancmange. I think we were entertained and given a balloon as well as the treasured Jubilee and Coronation mugs. I seem to recall sports events on the school field with the older youths and adults running races of all descriptions. I can still remember seeing fellows racing up and down the steep slope that is at the end of the field and at the side of the road running over the railway towards Oxford. Clearly what I observed at such a tender age was incomprehensible yet the memory still remains clear in terms of how I felt in the midst of the whirl of activity and energy from children and adults much older than I was at the time. I kept the mugs for many a year but never recall having drunk from either as they were considered to be special and only for admiration.

I now realise that somehow this somewhat lone existence is different from the present day experience of younger children who spend much of their pre-school years either at playgroup or in a day nursery. Much of my contact with people was essentially with adults particularly when accompanying my mother shopping both in Moreton and at other places such as Evesham, Oxford, Cheltenham and Stratford-upon-Avon. However, I am grateful for the fact that even during these early years I was being prepared for my vocation as a social scientist where so much of researching is based on what is termed 'participant observation'. The next step was for me to develop more interactive and social skills with a variety of other children, which was realised when time came to go to school, which leads on to the next phase of my childhood at Moreton.

Derrick Whitehouse

Moreton-in-Marsh High Street in the 1930s

Perhaps one of the most striking features of Moreton-in-Marsh is the long, wide and majestic High Street. It has always been at the centre of community life and today it is overwhelmed with traffic and the hustle and bustle of life in the 21st century.

In the 1930s it had its mad moments on market days and the annual fair plus a few special occasions but for most of the week it was tranquil with just the odd vehicle coming and going and the locals conducting their business in a gentle un-hurried way.

The following photographs are intended to present some nostalgia for those who were around at that time and insights for those who have arrived more recently on how life used to be in this beautiful town. The architecture harmonises through a varied collection of styles for the rich and those less affluent when the whole length of the street was adorned on both sides with mature and impressive lime trees.

I 'spect I grow'd

Derrick Whitehouse

Chapter two

The Infant school years from 1937 to 1940

I still have reasonably vivid memories of my first day at the Infants School. My parents must have prepared me well for the experience, as I am not aware that I encountered any anxiety about the first day, which may also have had some bearing on how I was greeted by Miss Gray the reception class teacher and the friendliness of the other children. I do remember that John Righton (who farms at Dorn) was also a new boy that day. The infant School at that time was in what was in its day a purpose built construction, which still stands at the end of Oxford Street. It consisted of a house for the head teacher integral with the three classrooms with screens so that the whole area could be made into one large room. There was a modest walled playground with the far end covered for wet weather. As with all schools in those days there were outside toilets.

For some reason still unknown to me I did not start school until I was five years old although it may have had something to do with the fact that at 4 ½ I had succumbed to a nasty bout of tonsillitis. However, I recollect that there were several younger children who in the afternoons were put to have a rest period on camp beds. Fortunately those of us who were a small group and a bit older, had the undivided attention of the teacher for a while to get us started on word and number recognition.

Derrick Whitehouse

I have the feeling now that I did not spend too long in the reception class but 'moved up' into the second class with Mrs Gray (no relation) where reading and number work started in earnest. In those days we initially used sand trays and slates to write on or in. I am aware that at the time I was slow at learning to read, which caused some anxiety for me and for my parents. With my present knowledge I now look back and realise that I suffered from a mild form of dyslexia, which was unheard of in those times. However, it proved something of a handicap for the rest of my school days.

Those first two years at the infant school embraced a tranquil period for everyone. It could be said it was the calm before the storm. At such a tender age we were all oblivious to what was happening on the international scene when we lived a peaceful life in this small market town in the Cotswolds.

At school I was not doing too badly and moved on to the top class formerly with Miss Clayton then with Miss Clements the new Head teacher, which coincided with the events leading up to the outbreak of the Second World War. The onset of hostilities meant that children from London (Mile End Road) were evacuated and Moreton played its part in providing hospitality. Consequently, the number of additional children to take in overwhelmed the schools. The result of this was that when the time came to move up to the Junior School several of us were held back to stay longer with the infants. At the time I did not understand what was going on and felt that there was something wrong with me. In addition we were being taught by teachers from London. However, they were very good at getting a move on with both basic arithmetic and spelling,

I 'spect I grow'd

which when we did move up to the Junior School we found that we were in fact ahead of those who had progressed in advance of us.

It probably goes without saying that around that time there were plenty of other distractions outside school to keep us occupied. When it came to marching (my passion at that time) in the months leading up to the Second World War I was enthralled as I watched the various groups on parade in the High Street. The Old Post Office, mentioned earlier in chapter one and next door to the Bell Inn, was now the depot for the local Territorial Army, which meant that the parking area in the High Street was the parade ground. Similarly the lads of the Air Training Corps were regularly parading up and down. Then for a brief period Moreton played host to the Green Howards regiment, which meant that there was marching with a band playing that was even more exciting for this young lad who by now at an age of rising six or seven was absolutely entranced with the glamour of forces parading. Before embarking for France the Green Howards were inspected by King George the Sixth himself. Naturally, all the school children were 'on parade' as well to cheer the King and his regiment. Sadly it was not long before I was observing troops returning from Dunkirk for resettlement before returning to their duties in some other war zone.

At my age it was hard to understand the full significance of being at war. However, I do recall having to be fitted with a gas mask. The whole population seemed to descend on what was then called 'The Senior School' (Now the Church Centre) on one or two evenings where we had to wait patiently seemingly forever, in a long queue to get fitted by a small army of helpers. I recall it was Tom Pye who fitted me out with a mask that we then had to carry with us wherever we went.

Also at the time when we were expecting war to be declared there was feverish activity in the High Street with fear that German bombers would soon be roaring overhead and dropping bombs. Therefore the RDC offices in particular had to be protected from the blast, which led to a time of filling hundreds of sandbags. For the youngsters it was tantamount to having a trip to the seaside when lorry loads of sand were deposited in the middle of the High Street. There was no shortage of young helpers as the photograph (see Chapter one) probably taken around the day war broke out illustrates (my father's Hudson Terraplane car, registration number AWP 59, is in the background). .

During the early years of WW2 there was always something happening that seemed spectacular for one so young. Those who were around at that time will remember the various weeks that were promoted to raise morale as well as put cash into the coffers to aid the war effort. There was *Dig for Victory Week, War Weapons Week,* and *Spitfire Week* all of which involved displays of marching and aerobatics over the town. I distinctly remember the thrill of seeing a Gloster Gladiator performing aerial manoeuvres above our heads.

I 'spect I grow'd

At around this time the Royal Air Force airfield was under construction, which was not particularly exciting until the first aircraft moved in. Now life really started to look up with a Hurricane squadron moving in first of all with lots of low flying. This was so different from the pre-war days when should an aircraft fly over, which was not too frequent the whole population would be out gazing skywards in rapt amazement.

When going near the airfield early on one could not help but notice that once the runways, dispersal points and buildings had been laid down the rest of our wonderful Moreton heathland had turned into a quagmire of mud. I understand that it was these appalling conditions that led Richard Murdock and Kenneth Horne (who I believe the latter was the Adjutant for a time) to label the RAF Station *Much Binding in the Marsh* (to 'bind' being the RAF war-time expression for whingeing or moaning). As most readers will know this heralded later a very successful radio show, which ran for several years.

It was shortly after Dunkirk that we had to move from the house next to the Council Offices to make way for expansion in office space. We were fortunate as we were asked to move just as Bill and Lillian Fry moved from the house (now called Wayside) to take over the Nursery gardens in Todenham Road. Consequently we moved in to the house further up the High Street, which continued to provide me with an observation post for what was happening throughout the War years and beyond.

It was about this time that I had my first bicycle. It was brand new with a carrier and a stand that allowed it to be stood upright and I could turn the pedals to make the back wheel spin whilst stationary – it was made by a company called Hopper. Once I could ride it meant that I could accompany my mother to her parent's home at Campden Ash five miles away. Gradually I became competent enough to cope with the hills at Bourton-on-the-Hill and Kennel Hill, which eventually led to dare devil rides to see how far one could ride down each hill without applying the brakes. Remember, that in these times there was very little traffic around. However, I do recall in the early days riding directly into an elderly gentleman walking along the road by the quarry at the top of Bourton-on-the-Hill to the great embarrassment of my mother.

For many years Evelyn Whitehouse was a familiar figure on her bicycle with her dog Bubbles in the basket traveling between Moreton and Campden Ash via Bourton-on-the- Hill. The Journey of five miles in each direction was undertaken in all winds and weather. The handle bars of the cycle were often weighed down with heavy bags either to take food and other items to her parents or carrying garden and farms produce home for own consumption.

I spent a great deal of my early life at Campden Ash where there was everything for an inquisitive young boy to enjoy. Mind you these days with health and safety regulations I realise that every time I went out on my own I was entering a world littered with hazards just waiting for accidents to happen. There were sheds with farm machinery with menacing cutting blades, which I climbed all over. I still shudder now when I remember the chaff cutter the huge handle of which we would spin round at great speed with uncovered blades that could have chopped off a limb if we got in the way. Then there was the opportunity to climb – sometimes on a hayrick, straw bales or the wonderful trees in the adjacent woods.

Needless to say it was not all hazardous and as with all life on the farm it was seasonal. I rode on the Suffolk punch horses or the carts they pulled. During the winter months dressed in sweaters, a scarf that was wrapped round and pinned at the back plus a woolly balaclava I was all set to go to a 'bury' where we retrieved mangolds to feed to the sheep. During the lambing season I would go out with the shepherd and was introduced at an early age to the trials of bringing lambs into the world. Then later in the year it was sheep shearing when I sometimes got involved in carrying the rolled up fleece into the storage building. There was never a dull moment what with helping my grandmother to feed the chickens, ducks and geese and my grandfather to feed the pigs that they kept in the sty and perhaps the worst thing of all watch as they were slaughtered. After this gruesome event I would watch my grandmother preparing every piece of the animal for consumption in some form or other. This included the cleaning of the intestines to be boiled and turned into what was termed 'chitterlings' to be boiled and eaten cold with some mustard, other parts were turned into 'brawn' and for me the best 'faggots' in the world with fresh peas from the sumptuous garden. Another delicacy never to be forgotten, and never heard of today, was rook pie, which was available during the rook shooting season. Then in the days before myxamatosis rabbits were always on the menu. Add to all this eggs and home made butter it was hard to feel deprived of the good things in life especially during the period of the Second World War. I was extremely lucky to have lived where I lived and to have the experience of enjoying the life and the benefits of being on a farm.

Perhaps the big event of the year on the Springhill estate was the annual Christmas and New Year party at the 'Big House' owned by Captain and Mrs Hannay. Everyone who worked or who had worked on the estate was invited, which meant it was a large gathering. We all sat down to a meal in the Servants Hall to be followed by some form of entertainment (a Conjuror or 8mm film of life on the estate) and the distribution of presents to everyone. It was really a riotous affair where some people often had too much alcohol. However, it was all very amicable and proved to be a special event for everyone including the Hannay family.

This experience naturally embraced all of my childhood years and into teenage. These days children are taken to farms around the country if they are lucky and can gain much experience and pleasure from even a few days on the farm. For me it was part and parcel of my growing up in the Cotswolds, which in many ways I took for granted. However, when I look back I realise what an amazing experience it was for me to have during my formative years.

Chapter three

The Junior school years – aged seven to eleven from 1940 to 1944

Moving to a new school is always a significant event in one's life and can be quite traumatic. Certainly I was ready for the move to the Junior School as I explained earlier having been held back due to the outbreak of the Second World War. The evacuees were still with us, possibly in slightly reduced numbers as some had returned to London. Nevertheless St. David's Church of England Junior Mixed (CEJM as we always referred to it) was numerically bursting at the seams.

In some ways it was ironical that we should have evacuees with us from London when at Moreton we had German bombers overhead en route for Birmingham and Coventry. During the Battle of Britain we regularly heard the characteristic drone of the engines wondering who would be getting the raid on any particular night. Those of us who were around on the night when Coventry suffered will never forget the glow in the sky from the fires more than thirty miles away. Everyone living in Moreton High Street and elsewhere was out viewing the spectacle. Then to add to the experience some of the bombers failed to drop all the bombs on the designated target and let them go when returning over the Cotswolds. There was a string dropped in the Blockley / Springhill area, where one demolished a house at the junction of the five mile drive and the Blockley turning and my grandparents at Campden Ash had one fall by their clothes line leaving a crater but no explosion, which to this day makes me wonder if there is still an unexploded bomb lurking. One very frightening incident was when a bomber flew very low down the length of Moreton High Street. I think we were all expecting it to crash into the Town Hall but fortunately it pulled away just in time. However, the slipstream blew out the large shop windows of Strongs, tailors and men's outfitters, now an antique business. Afterwards there was conjecture that the pilot may have perceived the location as an airfield. The RAF station was certainly a prime target, as the Germans probably knew that our own bomber crews were being trained there for subsequent raids over Germany.

The purpose-built junior school building had four classrooms – two on the ground floor with a dividing screen and a similar layout above on the first floor. There were separate cloakrooms for boys and girls indoors and separate outside toilets. The boys' toilet had a large open space immediately above the urinal, which presented an opportunity for a competition to see if any of us were capable of projecting the 'stream' up and over the top on to anyone standing around on the other side – I hasten to add that few succeeded but many rose to the challenge. We also had separate playgrounds where the girls had a smooth tarmac surface for hopscotch and other activities, whereas the boys' playground was rough gravel. An iron railing was between the two areas so some communication was possible but not often exercised.

The girls appeared to be always playing sensibly with variations in skipping and skipping songs as well as hopscotch and other peaceful but competitive pastimes. However, for the boys it was out and out 'warfare' especially in the early days of the war when we had the local lads standing up for their rights against 'the London bug-squashers', which was what we called the evacuees. The euphemism for play was simply called 'charging', which was enacted with the locals at one end of the area and the evacuees at the other and on a given cry we rushed towards each other and attempted to take 'prisoners' back to our corner, which led to further skirmishes to free them. For a short while after arriving at the school, I along with one or two timid souls, were bystanders but it was not long before we entered the fray. At the end of 'playtime' we staggered dishevelled back to the classroom with clothes awry, sometimes torn but nobody ever commented – perhaps teachers were content that we were worn out and would not disrupt the learning. There were days when we played chain tag and other more civilised activities.

In those times, and perhaps still the case in many schools we had seasonal pursuits. Common to both boys and girls we had a marbles season and a spinning top season. The onset of these activities was the result of what was in stock at Mace's shop (at the bottom end of the High Street near the Manor House Hotel). Mrs Mace ran the shop where all the play-things were sold along with sweets especially sherbet, which I have never liked. Mr Mace known as 'Snob' (a term for a cobbler or shoe mender) was in the adjacent room repairing foot-ware, but would occasionally appear with an impish face similar looking to how pixie craftsmen are depicted in a movie.

In the autumn we had 'conkers' mostly for the boys when we gathered the horse chestnuts from the trees along the Bourton-on-the-Hill road (sadly now many no longer there). At that time the Landgate fields had two quite large dew-ponds where we would find toads, newts and frogs. Another place for catching small fish was the brook running alongside the railway line between the Warwick Road bridge and Dorn where there were always stickleback to be found.

We were all greatly influenced by the films we saw and *The Count of Monte Cristo,* which encouraged a sword fighting season was a case in point. Our swords were wood with cardboard protection for the hand. For most of us the wooden swords were made from willow branches, which meant an expedition to the withy beds, an area reached from the

Evenlode Road turning off towards the bridge over the railway leading to Dunstall Farm. The withy beds were to the left before crossing the bridge. The withies were slender and when shaved presented us with a tapered and flexible sword. The amazing thing, compared with how things are today with health and safety plus playground supervision, was that we had pitched sword-fighting battles in the playground and nobody ever told us to stop. We even took our weapons into school and either deposited them under our desks or left them in the cloakroom ready for the next engagement after school.

The first class in the school was on the ground floor and my teacher was Miss Kay Smith, who was the only teacher I ever had a crush on. This was a time for engaging positively with the three Rs. Most afternoons we had reading groups and I always tried hard to stand next to Miss Smith. For a short time we had a student teacher Zoe Brown who used to take us on to the girls playground for drill and playground ball skills. Once or twice she even took us to the field at the Senior School for football. Being in this class was very pleasant. However, we had to brace ourselves for moving up the following year to Miss Hart's class, which was a different regime altogether.

Miss Hart was a martinet of the 'old' school and we were petrified at the prospect of moving up. She had a long dress almost to her ankles and hair tied back in a bun. The one thing that amused all of us was that she would bend over to place her handkerchief in the leg of her knickers under the elastic. Most mornings first thing we had scripture, which always seemed to be the reciting of the Catechism until we became word perfect. The section that I now recall with some amusement was the response to "*What did your godfathers and godmothers do then for you?*" "*They did promise and vow three things in my name – first that I should renounce the devil and all his works – the pomp's and vanities of this wicked world and all the sinful lusts of the flesh*". How could we all know what this really meant at the tender age of eight years? – but that was the way of the world at that time. Scripture was usually followed by chanting our tables and arithmetic followed by English, either reading or writing. On one or two mornings we would have singing, which would start with chanting over and over the tonic solfa – doh, ray, me, fah, et cetera. Then we would learn a song – the only one I can remember was the one about the young girl whose father was 'mowing the barley' and she finished up happily married to a lawyer and dwelling in 'a station above her'. What incredible messages we were being presented with. A tuning fork was used to launch us in with the right note.

The afternoon always started with spelling. This was usually done in turn round the class when if you got your word wrong you stood around the side of the class until everyone or most were standing. Then those standing were tested once again so that if you got your word correct you could sit down with great relief. It was sad and humiliating for those who were not bright as Miss Hart would explode often bashing the spelling into their heads with a twelve-inch ruler. Then on at least one afternoon each week we would close the afternoon with either handwork or drawing. Handwork always seemed to be about fashioning something out of a rectangle of coloured paper, which we did step by step under the instruction of the teacher – it was really an exercise in measuring and drawing lines with a ruler. The other afternoons ended with a story being read to us. The only two I can remember, and maybe that was our lot, were from *Tales of Troy and Greece* about either the adventures of Ulysses or the Trojan Horse story and John Bunyan's *Pilgrims Progress*. Miss Hart lived at Adlestrop with her mother, travelling to Moreton daily on the train. I suppose in that old fashioned way we all learned the basics of the three Rs from her. She would turn crimson with rage when we were being particularly dense. Therefore, it was not too surprising and sad, when about a year after leaving the Junior School we heard she had died from a heart attack whilst on Moreton Station platform.

The first class we entered upstairs was with Miss Isitt (who later became the owner and head of the private PNEU School) who was much more gentle in her approach to teaching. The work on spelling and writing as well as developing our arithmetic skills continued. There was more of an emphasis on our own personal responsibility. We were encouraged to select and read a variety of books either from the classroom store or the library box. Miss Isitt was artistic and encouraged rudimentary drama and more creative writing. The room had a piano, which meant that we had singing lessons with the teacher playing for us. The songs we sang were always very patriotic and included the words of *I vow to thee my country, Land of Hope and Glory* and Parry's *Jerusalem*. Once a week we had a BBC schools broadcast entitled *Singing Together* with a man called Herbert Wiseman. Another broadcast was for drill where we each stood in the gangway between the desks and performed the exercises. I now know, having trained as a Physical Education teacher, that these were from the 1933 Syllabus, which stipulated certain exercise routines to be performed during a particular week in the educational year and woe betide any teacher who transgressed from this pattern especially if an inspector came into the school.

I 'spect I grow'd

It was around this time that I started to stay for school dinners instead of going home. In terms of my own social education this was a sensible move as it provided me with an opportunity to eat with other children. I recall that it was not simply with children of my own age but we sat with the much older young people from the senior school where we had to go for the meal. It brings to mind sitting with a girl called Norma from Todenham who looked after me very well and was near to leaving secondary school.

At the end of the year those who were seen to have ability progressed to the 'top' scholarship class with the Headteacher Miss Philpot. Some scholarship children passed the eleven plus first time whilst others took it a second time a year later. Alas I was in the latter category and I can now admit that I failed the exam both times. I was a nervy child suffering regularly from tonsillitis, which resulted in my increased anxiety and desire to succeed. This meant that each time I was due to take the exam I developed acute stomach pains and came to school doubled up in agony. However, in those days, before the 1944 Education Act, Chipping Campden Grammar School was a fee-paying establishment and for the first year of secondary education my parents paid for me to be a pupil. The absurdity of all this and my long standing criticism of the 11+ is that on the first day at the Grammar School I was given a test in both maths and English without warning and was promptly put into the 'A' stream where I came third in the first set of marks for the term.

I put down my ability to achieve this level to the expertise and diligence of Miss Philpot who again was one of the old school of teachers with a dress to the ankles and hair in a bun. For two years we were worked hard at improving in English and essay writing as well as every afternoon grinding through page upon page of arithmetic, decimals, fractions, long division and multiplication. The result of this was that when the Moreton children arrived at the Grammar School we were way ahead of the children from the other feeder schools. However, there was some respite from all this hard work especially when Miss Philpot's companion and housekeeper would come in at the end of the day to read to us. The story I best remember was *The Black Arrow,* which recounted the adventures of Dick Shelton and the heroine Joanna Sedgely. This was 'great stuff' feeding the spirit of adventure and justice in all of us. It proved so popular that we had it read to us more than once.

Being a Church School meant that at certain times in the ecclesiastical year we were in church. The obvious one was St. David's Day, which was followed by a half-day holiday and at festival times such as Easter, Ascension Day and Christmas. At Christmas we presented a Nativity Play when, on the one occasion I participated, I appeared, much to my disgust, as an angel. However, even at this late stage in my life I can remember the opening words of the play spoken by the principal characters:

Joseph (played by Bill Beacham) – *Mary art thou the little maid who plucked me flowers in spring? – I know thee not – I feel afraid – thou art strange this evening.*

Mary (played by Dola Spittle) – *A stranger came with feet of flame and told me this strange thing – for all I am is a village maid – my son shall be a King.*

My parents were not churchgoers but with hindsight perhaps the most meaningful spiritual occurrence for me at this time was when I attended Harvest Festival with my mother. During the week at school Miss Isitt who had suggested we should ask parents to take us to the service had told us about the importance of harvest. As an obedient child and with a dutiful parent we attended. It was held in the evening and we entered the church where there was subdued lighting and all the produce beautifully laid out at the front of the church. I had never experienced such a wonderful glowing picture, which has remained with me all my life. In fact I now tell people that this was probably the first step I took on my personal spiritual journey.

All that has been described so far was school but there were many other things to contend with in my life at this time and I was all set to tackle a steep learning curve in my social and community learning. The reader is asked to remember that this was during the Second World War and as a child I was surrounded by a culture that was about war. Now I look back I realise that what encircled me appeared to be glamour and adventure of all things military. By that token it is possible for me to understand how today boys in third world countries can easily be recruited as boy soldiers as in a less dramatic form this is exactly what happened to me.

For a while the army had left to go to the front or to fire antiaircraft guns at enemy planes as they flew over. At the same time the RAF station was only just getting underway. All that was left was the local Boy Scout Troop with members often seen charging around with their scout poles at the ready. In addition there was the formation of the local company of the

Home Guard. At the time this was enough to fire my imagination and enthusiasm.

I longed to become a Scout but at the age of eight was far too young and there was no wolf cub pack at that stage. However, every time we went to Oxford to shop with my mother I pestered her to take me to the Scout Shop in The Turl where each time we purchased either a *Scout Diary, The Wolf Cub Handbook* or finally *Scouting for Boys,* both the latter having been written by Robert Baden-Powell. The two books were my bedtime reading either by me or aloud by my mother. It was enthralling to be captivated by the spirit of exploration and service presented by B-P. The idea of camping, and in place of a shower, rolling in the dew-covered grass in the early morning was very appealing. B-P also told us that the definition of a gentleman was someone who had clean toenails (not too sure about that one but I was impressed at the time). From a practical point of view I sat and learned all the knots and lashings, semaphore and Morse code along with other valuable facts.

An opportunity emerged that enabled me to consolidate on some of this learning. Members of the Home Guard used to meet every Sunday Morning for training at the British Legion in Station Road, and presented an occasion not to be missed initially for observation and later modest participation. I recall they met at around 10-00 a.m. but I was always hanging around in readiness by 9-30. For some unknown reason no other boys seemed to have a similar interest in what was going on and in the course of time I appear to have become an unofficial mascot for the company. This was made more manifest when my parents managed to acquire a small army tunic and forage cap, which I wore with great pride every Sunday morning. Also to enhance my understanding of weaponry it was possible to purchase booklets on the various guns. Consequently I devoured the information on the Lewis gun, the Bren gun and the Thompson Machine gun and I was all set to strip down and assemble any of these deadly pieces of equipment.

I 'spect I grow'd

The training sessions began with everyone coming on parade with details for the session being presented by Sergeant Major Williams. The Commanding Officer was Major Freer who lived at Stretton-on-Fosse. It seemed that NCO status was given to anyone who had served in the First World War according to rank and experience then with a possible upgrade for the Home Guard. Presumably Williams had been a senior NCO whereas others may have been more lowly, perhaps even privates or lance corporals. Following the gathered parade they divided into groups according to specialism. Some went off to practice rifle drill, bayonet drill or throwing hand grenades. Two groups that I latched on to were the machine gun team and the signallers. They stayed near the British Legion. Initially I watched and learned, then later if a team member was missing for any reason, I was asked to join in the drill or practice. The machine gun team was under the charge of Corporal Percy Lloyd (local shoe sales and repairs in Oxford Street) who had served with the Machine Gun Corps in WW1. Everything was performed on commands, by numbers, to assemble the gun and make ready for action. This entailed presenting the stand, fixing the gun, putting ammunition boxes for the gunner to sit on then loading ready to fire. The other group was the signallers under the direction of Corporal Billy Allen (local carpenter and undertaker) with his son Jim (later to excel as goalkeeper and wicket keeper for Moreton teams) father of the present undertaker Peter Allen. Normally Jim and Eric Norledge would take themselves off to the top of the bank near the railway bridge over the Oxford road. Signalling in both Morse and semaphore would then take place between them and Billy in the grounds of the Legion. I would frequently assist in reading messages or writing them down. Naturally, I was never asked to send but am sure I could have risen to the challenge. There was another time when I followed the company to the firing range at Hinchwick Warren (a mile or two beyond Bourton-on-the-Hill) and to the range at the RAF station. I vividly remember the latter occasion when everyone had a chance to fire a Tommy Gun, which was thrilling.

Derrick Whitehouse

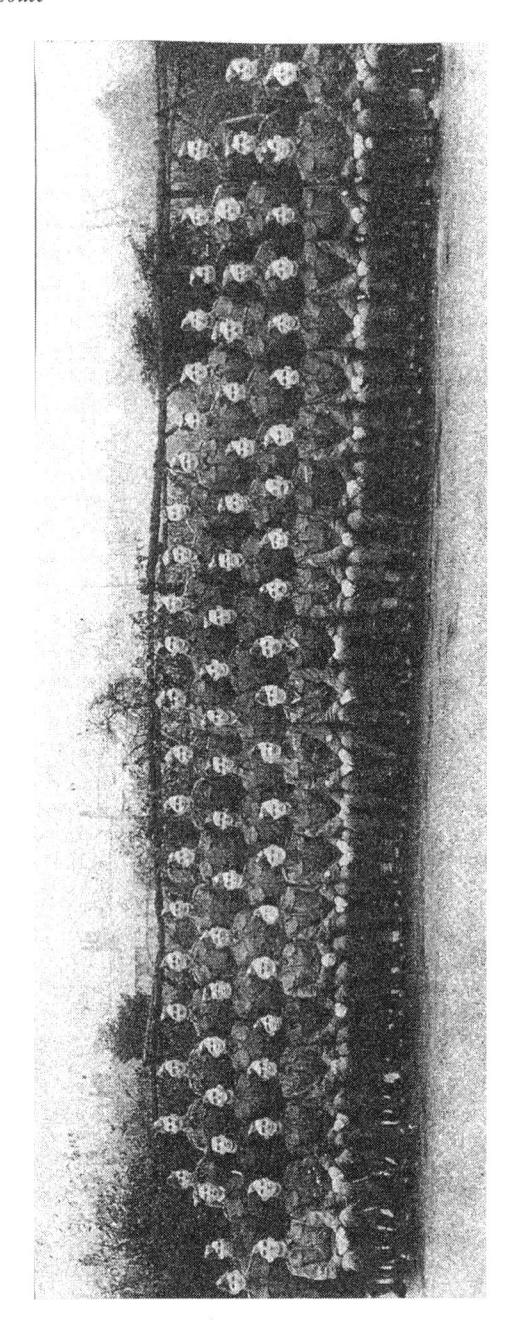

Moreton Home Guard Company – Taken around 1943 / 44

I 'spect I grow'd

I cannot help remembering that the instruction was to fire bursts of around five rounds at one time. However, Tommy Coxhill (local road sweeper and step-father to David whom I will talk about later) simply kept his hand on the trigger with the result that the gun rose higher and higher into the air much to the amusement of everyone and with Tommy almost finishing up on his back. Another local character in the Home Guard was Billy Howells who together with his father, also Billy, manufactured fences, gates and hurdles for farmers. The workshop and outdoor area was in Old Town near the church and on the corner entering Warneford place. They were both cheerful and amusing folks. There was also Ken Hope the head forester for the Batsford estate. Later he was adviser to Moreton Parish Council on the management of trees in the town. I have very fond memories of these times and how I came to be accepted by the men especially as now and again when they had finished and retired to the bar one of them would appear with a glass of lemonade for me as a thank you and maybe saying 'you are one of us'.

In February 1941 Lord Baden-Powell founder of the Scout Movement died. In May of that year a Wolf Cub Pack was started in Moreton and I was on the doorstep desperate to join. The Cub Mistress or Akela was Mrs Dyer the Manageress of the Progressive Laundry in London Road (now demolished) and wife of Bill Dyer the Group Scoutmaster who was away at the War in the RAF. The Scout Hut, a wooden, possibly ex-army, construction (on the site of the present Scout HQ) had been commandeered to house soldiers. Consequently, the makeshift Scout Hut was a two storey garage in School Road (now a single storey garage and smaller) belonging to Andrew Horne. When I think back now I realise that these days the building would be condemned for health and safety reasons but not then. The ground floor was a garage with rickety steps to the floor above where there was an open space. The floor was sprung like a trampoline with little or no reasonable support.

So just imagine a group of boisterous boys charging up and down or doing Morris Dancing, which was one activity we tried as cubs. This was our home till the end of hostilities.

I am not sure just how many there were of us on that first night but I estimate between 20 and 30. At that stage I was a rising nine year old but we were not divided in Sixes straight away, as we needed to be sorted out. We were introduced to what cubbing was all about and taught all the things we needed to know in order to be invested as tenderpads (tenderfoot for Scouts). Naturally for all I have explained earlier I was in my element and when it came to organising us into Sixes I was made Seconder to Ronny Hartley an older boy and very much the tough leader of the gang at school and elsewhere. When it came to competitions between the Sixes we always won largely due to my already acquired expertise in a number of skill areas. This was a breakthrough in terms of the development of my esteem in the group as a whole. At school I was now very much one of the gang.

Once we got going Mrs Dyer was helped by some of the senior scouts who entertained us and organised quizzes, knot tying races and signalling competitions. On one occasion Flying Officer Fred Walker joined us; he had been a scout, and had recently returned from the USA where he had gained his wings as a pilot. He was in his RAF uniform and led us all in singing *The boys of the Army Aircorp.* Some readers will know the first few words, *"Off we go in the wild blue yonder"* – sadly it was only a short while later that Fred Walker was shot down in his bomber and killed. I am so glad that I have this memory of him as he visited and inspired a group of young lads during those troubled times.

I 'spect I grow'd

Flying Officer Fred Walker – Bomber Pilot and former Moreton Scout. Killed in action on a bombing raid 1942.

The one big outing we had as cubs was a trip to the pantomime Cinderella at the Alexandra Theatre in Birmingham. We travelled by train to Honeybourne Junction then took the other line to Birmingham Snow Hill Station. This was a great event for all these country boys who had no experience of a city. We must have walked through Birmingham with our mouths wide open to see trams and trolley buses for the first time as well as the damage from the bombing. Quite an adventure for us in those days.

Time passed and individuals either moved on to become scouts or felt that being a cub was not for them. Those of us who stayed on gradually moved up through the ranks and when it was time for me to move up to join the scouts I was Senior Sixer with various stars and badges.

One of the things that people of my generation remember about our childhood is that we had so much more freedom and less supervision. My parents were caring but allowed me to roam and they did not discriminate on the range of friendships I had. Now I look back I realise the potential hazards that existed both in terms of possible injury as well as actions that could have got me into trouble. As a result I wandered far and wide around the town and the surrounding countryside with various individuals.

Derrick Whitehouse

I have already mentioned David Coxhill who lived with his mother and stepfather in a flat in New Road. David's mother was eccentric in her appearance and behaviour, maybe a latter-day flapper. She had long red hair and wore dresses that were unconventional for the time. She encouraged David to be unusual, particularly in that for a boy he grew his red hair down to his shoulders, which was unheard of at the time. (When he was around 14 years of age he had it slightly shorter). David was a very intelligent boy and it was often rumoured that his father was Russian (possibly a prince – but that may have been a myth). He was wild to an extreme and even as a young lad could often be seen walking on the roof of the building. I remember seeing him there one day with an orange box and some planks of wood saying that he was going to build an aeroplane. (Shades of the Colditz story of later years). He was older than me but I would often go to his home to join in with some of his antics. They had a piano and though not taught he could sit down and play anything by ear. I recall that his speciality was *Lady be good,* which was our way of having a jam session. Another pastime with David and another rascal Roy Walker was to cross over the road to the building, now the WI centre of operations, which was at that time derelict cottages and used for storing bales of waste paper. This was just the place to have a secret den in the midst of the dozens of bales. How we never set fire to the whole lot I shall never know.

Further mischief was to embark on expeditions with air rifles and pistols. An extension to the RAF station accommodation for the women of the WAAF, now WRAF, was built adjacent to the Bourton-on-the-Hill Road (now the Caravan Park). However, our way towards the buildings was across the Landgate fields and as we approached the WAAF quarters we would be crawling on our bellies with great stealth. The target was the smalls hanging on the lines to dry. I leave the reader to picture what we got up to with our air weapons. Although very intelligent David

I 'spect I grow'd

never went to the Grammar School but was educated at the Roman Catholic all-age school at Chipping Campden. When he became a teenager he joined the Moreton Army cadets, which probably gave him a taste for real guns. This was to herald his demise. Around this time the US forces were at Moreton with a Railway Transport Officer (RTO) operating from a tin shed at the Railway Station. David could get in anywhere and somehow he broke into the RTO's shed and took the American Carbine rifle with ammunition. The following morning he was found dead in bed with the rifle by his side. The Coroner presented an Open Verdict on this tragedy. This maverick but fascinating young man left quite a gap in the youth culture of Moreton at that time and I still remember him fondly as he may have been instrumental in turning me into something of a nonconformist and radical in my own future life.

We had dens everywhere, usually in the undergrowth of woodland areas. Our favourite place where many of us would congregate to engage in mock warfare of one sort or another was what we called the 'Rec.' woods, which are now referred to by the more up-market title of the Queen Victoria Recreation Ground. One time it would be English and Germans then cowboys and Indians and sometimes we would be Anzacs when we wore what were sold as cowboy hats but we would turn up one side. In those times the whole area was overgrown to present many hiding places with a network of paths. We gave the various sections of the wooded area numbers in order to control where those hiding would be located. The first wood was the short stretch from the gate entrance to the park in Batsford Road up to the House at the entrance to the cricket ground. The second wood was from the House to the bridge leading from the recreation ground to the cricket field. Then the third wood, the largest area, ran from the cricket field bridge to the bridge entering Hospital Road. Finally, the fourth wood ran from the third across the brook and adjacent to the cricket field up to the tennis courts. At the outset of our hostilities we would agree on for example, second and third wood only, which we all conformed to. Trees were readily climbed and the undergrowth offered many opportunities to hide.

Another favourite pastime when the brook was reasonably high was to have races with makeshift boats usually from the cricket field bridge to the end where the stream enters the tunnel to come out by the railway station. So! Where did we get the boats? At that time the fencing surrounding the railway station was made from pointed wooden struts three to four feet in height and when removed looked remarkably like ideal boats for the race. For a long time the fence had many gaps in its length. We were fairly discreet as we usually had a special hiding place for our boat in readiness for the next race. Another boat experience was at the swings, which these days would never pass health and safety regulations. The boat was a large structure that could be crammed with several young bodies often around six or even eight bodies. The object then was to work it up so that it would be swinging horizontally with the top girder over the swing area. As far as I know nobody ever fell out or off this wild but exciting activity. The seesaw, which was long and hefty, made from half tree trunk, was similarly abused enabling large numbers, crowded the whole length to enjoy collective enjoyment. When it was wet we would congregate in one of the two summer houses. On the lazy days of summer a special place to lie down, reflect and share was to bask in the sunshine on the roof of the old cricket pavilion. We gained access by climbing up the sight screens resting at the rear of the building. These were our *Cider with Rosie* years and gave us a great sense of belonging.

Another favourite place for playing secretly was the whole area of the railway station. There were sidings everywhere adjacent to the station itself but also running from beyond the Oxford road bridge past the school field to end up alongside the Junior School playground leading to Warneford Place where lorries

I 'spect I grow'd

could come alongside trucks to load and unload. Chasing round and climbing in and out of the trucks became another favourite pastime when we usually arrived home filthy from coal dust or whatever.

A further attractive place for exploration in one way or another had to be the RAF station, which was surrounded by a barbed wire fence and was a definite deterrent. However, we made the best of opportunities that were presented. For most of the wartime period the station was an Operational Training Unit (OTU) with the task of training crews on Wellington bombers, which meant that crews were engaged in flying on operations and sadly the RAF cemetery reflects this when one looks at the tombstones bearing the names of young men lost during operational flying. Along the London road on the side of the road near the present industrial estate was a pillbox sunk into the ground but rising with a flat top a few feet above the surface and right at the end of the main runway. It needs no imagination to see that this presented Moreton youngsters with a vantage point to observe the taking off and landing of aircraft. We would stand on top of the pillbox waving our arms as we saw a plane starting the take off and then we would flatten ourselves as the bombers roared just feet above our heads. No one ever suggested this could be dangerous or reprimanded us for taking such a risk.

I had a friend at school probably a year or two older than me called Basil Body who lived within the boundary of the airfield on Todenham Road. His father was the Clerk of Works for the Air Ministry at Moreton. Quite often Basil would invite me to accompany him to his house with the intention of exploring the airfield. There was a guarded gate on the Todenham Road and Basil had a special pass but would say to the guard that I was his friend who was coming to play. The way the aircraft were parked was to spread them out over a wide area at dispersal points in case of being bombed. This meant crossing

Derrick Whitehouse

the Todenham road into the fields where the ground crews would work on the aircraft to prepare them for the next flight. Just imagine two boys wandering along and admiring at close range these monsters. We would sidle up to the ground crew and ask what they were doing and attempt to ask intelligent questions. Eventually, we would either ask or be invited to have a look inside – Yes! That was just what we wanted. As well as Wellingtons there were also other smaller aircraft – I recall climbing into a Westland Lysander and an Avro Anson. At other times at night I would watch from the attic window of our house in Moreton High Street the bombers lining up on the perimeter track to take off on night bombing raids, when some did not return.

As well as the locals going to the airfield the inhabitants of the RAF station came to us. Naturally when off duty the eight public houses in Moreton were used as a social venue for Airmen and members of the WRAF and in fine weather the surrounding fields with the long grass offered hospitality to courting couples.

That was dependent on whether or not they were approached by Mr Clifford (known to many as Coco Clifford) who owned a clothing shop but on a Sunday would lobby service personnel and encourage them to attend the Gospel Hall, which was then located near the railway siding. Sadly he lost his own son Tim (photographed) who was in the RAF during the Second World War. Stationed in Belgium he was servicing an aircraft when a German aircraft flew

I 'spect I grow'd

down machine gunning the aircraft on the ground – Tim standing no chance of escape.

From time to time the RAF Concert Party, comprised of both airmen and airwomen, would put on a show for the locals in our modest cinema located in Church Street now occupied by the Manor House Hotel. There was a great deal of talent exhibited, the owners of which were either professional entertainers or, post-war, became household names in the entertainment world.

Then quite soon after the USA had entered the War along came the Americans with a small detachment of Infantry. They were housed in the hutted complex known as the Territorial Camp (now Jameson Close) and the guards on the entrance wore the now outdated boy-scout type hats that we see the troops wearing in the films about Pearl Harbour. At that stage it was all a curiosity but many of the lads were there asking for 'any gum chum?' and being slipped bars of Hershey Chocolate and the original Coca Cola. Their stay was fairly short lived leading to a blank period until just before the Second Front was about to start. It was a little later that the Yanks turned up in force.

They were the American 6th Armoured Division under the command of General Patton. We could not miss them as their Sherman Tanks filled Moreton High Street (a painting and photographs can be seen and cards purchased at the Wellington Museum) and what a wonderful opportunity for all the local lads to make new friends. Several of us attached ourselves to one of the tank crews. In fact the one I chose appears in one of the photographs at the Museum. What this meant to us was that we spent almost every spare moment with the crew. I would go riding on or in the tank when they went for fuel at the pump, which was where the Wellington Museum is now situated, called the British School. All the troops were accommodated in tents in what was then referred to as Tarplett's Field, which was just past the White Horse public house (now Inn on the

Marsh). We would spend time there and as well on several occasions lined up for 'chow' food with them and ate beef with sauerkraut for the first time. Naturally we were overwhelmed with chewing gum, Hershey bars and Coca Cola. Then they were gone, only to be seen in action via the newsreels at the cinema. There was some *quid pro quo* as we invited some of the tank crew to our homes for some English hospitality. Very significant memories remain but sadly I never met up with any of them later although I know some have visited Moreton in more recent times but alas I was elsewhere.

The Sherman tank crew that befriended this young lad

After the US forces had left it meant that the vacated army camps at Bourton-on-the-Hill and on the Springhill Estate were empty – but not for too long. Once D Day had taken place the German prisoners moved in and had to be housed somewhere. Consequently both sites were turned into internment camps. This event presented further opportunities for experience and learning. At Springhill where my grandparents lived there was interaction with the prisoners. On occasions I accompanied a

I 'spect I grow'd

farm worker (Tom Stanley who lodged with my grandparents) with his cart drawn by Suffolk Punch horses to the camp to collect food waste for pig swill. We would enter through the main gate to go to the cookhouse for our cargo. Initially I was quite scared having been fed with weird tales about our enemies but soon realised they were the same as us. In fact some selected prisoners were set to work on the farm. I clearly remember one prisoner called Peter who was obviously well educated with perfect English (I would have liked to know his profession) and a lovely person to talk with. One activity that emerged quite soon was a form of barter between the locals and the prisoners. The trading was for cigarettes in the main and the prisoners, many of whom were skilled craftsmen would produce ships in bottles, scenes in clear light bulbs (still have one), wooden models and slippers made from blankets. A very special event I bring to mind was a classical music concert given by an orchestra of German prisoners in the Astra Cinema at the RAF station. I recollect reading the programme, which not only set out the music but listed all the players and their background most of whom had played in the top orchestras in Germany and Austria. That was my first introduction to hearing live orchestral classical music.

It was the pattern at the time for prisoners to be moved on, often to Canada, which meant that they had to be moved at night for transit from the camps to the railway station at Moreton. The reader is now asked to imagine being wakened at around two in the morning with in fact rousing but accomplished singing of German military marching songs, which could be heard all the way from Bourton-on-the-Hill. Then they entered and queued along Moreton High Street waiting to embark. We looked out of our bedroom window to see masses of Germans patiently waiting with just a handful of guards. I was thrilled to hear the singing, but others were not amused and complaints were made and the singing stopped. All we would hear subsequently was the shuffle of people as they marched through the town, which was creepy and somewhat sinister.

Perhaps the favourite venue at that time was the Playhouse Cinema, which was located in Church Street where the auditorium part still exists and is used by the Manor House Hotel. People would flock in from the whole area. Buses ran from Stow-on-the-Wold and Bourton-on-the-Water as well as those who cycled in from other villages. The film changed twice a week and progressed to having a Sunday evening showing after church services had ended. The seat prices for adults were, 7 pence, 1s.10d and 2s. 6d. For children it was 4d, 10d and I think around 1s.3d for the best seats. The four-pennies was the place to be for all the kids. It was probably very slightly healthier to be there because the whole central area would be filled with cigarette smoke, which could be seen as it rose up through the beam from the projector to the screen. Later on towards the end of the war we had Saturday morning cinema with all the usual children's films for that period. The Playhouse was managed by Mrs G.M. Dee and her daughters Patricia and Brenda. The queues and general behaviour was handled effectively by Billy Eldridge whose daytime work was that of the local chimney sweep. Mrs Dee's youngest son Henry, though a little older, was a good friend. (He was known as Chick – probably given to him by older brother John because a small Hen was a chick). On many Saturday mornings I would accompany Chick to the Creamery to collect butter, eggs, cheese and milk for family consumption. This was an eye opener as we were able to see the production of butter and the processing of the milk coming from farms in churns to be transferred into tankers for the journey to London

One of the great attractions for living in Moreton, and I believe still could be, is that there is plenty of scope for walking and cycle rides, which does not mean having to retrace your steps in order to arrive home. In other words routes can be circular

I 'spect I grow'd

as well as offer either long or short expeditions. We could walk across the Dorn fields or cycle up the Batsford Road along to Dorn and home via the Fosseway for example. However, there are several other possibilities and we made the most of them. These included round trips to Evenlode and Broadwell or Todenham and Wolford. Sometimes a group of us would set off whilst on other occasions it would be just two or even alone. The great wish was always to get back home without getting a puncture. I think at that time rubber tyres and inner tubes were not up to present standards and some of us were not terribly good at mending punctures properly. Consequently many of our difficulties stemmed from old patches coming off. The condition of the roads did not always help. Another hazard was riding at night with lamps that had to be covered from above so as not to shine upwards and attract German bombers. Interestingly it was a serious offence to ride a bicycle without lights front and rear. Following the convening of the local magistrates court there was always a list in the local paper of those charged and fined for riding without lights. I think the local bobby would lurk in a shop doorway and emerge to catch people passing by without lights. Sometimes on bikes I would accompany my friend Peter Lloyd to deliver newspapers to Sezincote and Longborough where we would stop off to go exploring in the ground of the Manor. At other times I would go to Batsford to see another friend Barry Gerrard. His father was the chauffeur for Lord Dulverton but he was away in the RAF during the war and Barry and his mother were moved to a cottage in the kitchen garden. This location enabled Barry and I to go exploring in the area that is now the arboretum, which even at that time was quite a spectacle.

There was always something interesting to explore and in those turbulent times there was always something happening. The second front manifested as D Day came and we were enthralled by aeroplanes flying over with white stripes painted on the wings and we started to look forward to the end of hostilities. This coincided with the excitement of moving on to the Grammar School. We had heard a good deal of what to expect from those already there but we had a chance to experience something of what it was like when we were allowed to take time off from junior school to attend the Grammar School Sports Day. This was quite overwhelming as it was not only my first visit to the school but also I had never experienced so many children and young people en masse before. What was in prospect for us during the coming years in this new environment?

Chapter four

The Secondary School years from 1944 to 1950

Moving up to the Grammar School at Chipping Campden (CCGS) was towards the end of the Second World War during a time of shortage and making do. Clothes were rationed. Consequently there was no insistence on exact compliance with school uniform especially it seemed for boys but girls were expected to be kitted out with gymslips. As a makeshift effort for boys the school had got hold of some awful green caps but my mother managed to obtain one of the traditional caps in blue with gold bands from the mother of Alan Butt who had left and was now in the RAF. This I wore with pride on the back of my head and for years afterwards kept it in memory of my school days.

There were two ways of getting from Moreton to Campden, either by bus or train. Most of us went in two buses, which were always crowded but had a great spirit aboard often with singing all the way there and back. Each day one bus was left unlocked in the market square at Campden ready for the return journey. This provided an opportunity for some of us to go into town after school usually to buy cakes at James' shop on the corner of Sheep Street and High Street. I vividly remember an incident when I was dithering about which cake I wanted and was given short shrift by the woman serving to 'Make your b****y mind up'. Quite a shock but not unusual. We would then join the bus and wait to be taken home via picking up back at school. Later, probably for economic reasons, all of us from Moreton had to travel on the train, when just one bus ferried us from Campden

Station to school. Often some of us would simply walked the mile or so up the hill.

Photo from the collection of Geoffrey Powell

A regular rather quaint spectacle at Campden Station was what we schoolboys called *The Flying Greenhouse*, which was a vehicle owned by a spritely little man called George Haysum. Today we would call the bus a people carrier with seating for around eight people. However, it had a large box-like body with enormous windows but a small engine that sounded rather like a sewing machine – hence the greenhouse appearance. George plied his business for a few pence for those needing to get from the town to the station or from the station to the town. He always travelled down the hill towards the station but it is unlikely that the bus would make it back up the hill. Consequently for the return journey it went along towards the Campden / Paxford road where the incline was less then back to the town.

I 'spect I grow'd

Before the 1944 Education Act the Grammar School had a private school philosophy with fee payers as well as scholarship children. There were also two boarding houses with the boys in the old Grammar School in the High Street and the girls in Seymour House also in the High Street. Both groups would form a crocodile to march to school in the morning and for the girls after lunch as well. In the latter case during snowy weather the girls were sitting targets for snowballing dayboys.

When the 1944 Education Act became law the boarding section was closed and children who were either day-pupils or boarders who were not up to standard for a Grammar School form of learning seemed to disappear. Some boarders stayed on as dayboys. Most notable now were the Tolkein brothers, nephews of JRR (who had presided over an earlier Speech Day and recommended CCGS to his brother), who travelled in by train from Littleton and Badsey where the family were market gardeners. As I explained in a previous chapter my parents were initially fee payers but with the new legislation and the fact that I was deemed up to the mark a fee was no longer required, which was a relief for both me and my parents.

In this period prior to the end of WW2 the school was still heavily oversubscribed. It was just a two-form entry establishment but I observe from my old school reports that during the first two or three years the class sizes exceeded forty pupils, which put considerable pressure not only on the pupils but also on the teachers. I am now aware that because of the war with men away we had more women than men teaching us and I would venture to say that some of them were not especially well-qualified and had problems with discipline. As men and women returned from military service the short-term staff disappeared and better teachers were taken on.

When I look back after a lifetime in education I realise what a delightful school it was for the social education of young people. Naturally being co-educational was the key factor. Another influence was the size and despite the large classes the number of pupils probably did not exceed two hundred and fifty. There were two activities that played a significant part in this form of learning. First, there was dancing during the lunch period when there were two (later three) pianists, namely, a teacher Mr Fitzhugh and talented pupils John Archibald and later Albert Philips. In later years Albert Unstead (a new teacher) arrived with records and a record player, leading to further development of our repertoire and skills. The style for dancing was mainly old time with the *palais glide, valeta* and *military two-step*. Later we progressed to more modern dances e.g. *waltz, foxtrot* and *quickstep*. Initially as unimportant younger boys and shy with it, we would peep in or congregate near the entrance only to be pounced on by senior girls (I recall Georgina Attwood being one of them) and hauled round the Hall. It was not long before we had the courage and expertise to join in without hesitation. The second experience of unsupervised social education was during the sunny days of summer when the grass was long around the edge of the sports field and we would sit and lie around in mixed groups chatting and getting to know each other. Nobody ever came to supervise what was going on, which was quite innocent anyway. Towards the end of the autumn term just before Christmas we always had the socials (junior and senior), which were great events for dressing up. I recall wearing my first long trousers at one such event (at that time we all wore shorts until around age thirteen).

A novel feature at the top end of the playing field for several years was a redundant RAF Hurricane fighter. The school had an Air Training Corps (ATC) flight and the plane had somehow been acquired for training purposes. It was surrounded by barbed wire but often aircraft from RAF Moreton or elsewhere could be seen flying low overhead thinking that one of their own machines had come down. Lying in the long grass behind the aircraft was a secluded place for some of the older students during fine weather.

The designation of the classes was rather strange by present day standards and probably resembled terms embracing the public school image rather than those of state controlled establishments with As and Bs. We started in 1A and one remove (1R the B stream) then on to two Upper / 2U and two Lower / 2L followed by 3U and 3L, which in turn became 4U and 4L, finally rising for School Certificate or Matric to 5U and for some quirky reason 5R. The sixth form was normally referred to as first and second year being the standard time spent there for Higher School Certificate. I imagine that initially the Upper and Lower streams were based on English and mathematical ability then as one progressed up the school the division was based on ability in French. The final reckoning was that the remove class would focus on practical subjects like cookery and woodwork and withdraw from learning a modern language.

The school day always started with an assembly for everyone in the Hall (the only large space at that time). The format for the worship was the same every time. We started with a hymn followed by reciting as a school the *General Confession* from the Anglican Liturgy, which I now perceive as a subliminal form of disciplining the students having asked us to confess to having *erred and strayed like lost sheep.* We then had the *Lord's Prayer* and a reading plus a closing blessing. In those times this was a formalised ritual that brought us all together as a school and I believe had an impact on our developing a corporate sense of belonging.

A further connection with the Anglican liturgy was at around the age of thirteen when some of our parents felt that we should become confirmed into the Church of England. Consequently, around eight or maybe ten of us attended Confirmation classes at Moreton Rectory (now a private house) with Canon Ingham the Rector as our tutor. I am still not sure how seriously we felt about these sessions but it was a group event so we all went along with receiving instruction. However, I do remember that each time we were drilled in the words of a hymn, which we sang at the confirmation service – *Come Holy Ghost our souls inspire and brighten with thy Celestial fire.* Clearly these words have stayed with me till the present day and have probably had an influence on my spiritual thinking over the years.

For many years I became a regular communicant and in my thirties actually considered the possibility of applying for ordination. However, an incident shortly after confirmation leads me to believe that I was already beginning to question my future allegiance to the Anglican Church. Canon Ingham suggested that he would like me to become a server for the Communion services. I went to one session for instruction but then decided it was not for me. I now wonder if this was the beginning of change by rejecting ritual as an integral part of worship and my path towards becoming a Quaker was just beginning. I have now been worshipping with the Religious Society of Friends (Quakers) for nearly fifty years.

My first year at the Grammar School coincided with the end of hostilities in WW2. It also overlapped with my moving from being a wolf cub to becoming a boy scout, which also linked with the return of the Scout Hut for our usage. It was not long after this event that I found myself sitting leisurely on my bike at Moreton Town Hall watching the world go by when a small ambulance from the RAF station drew up and out got a Squadron Leader Medical Officer. He came towards me and asked if there was a local scout troop. I gave him details of where we met and at what time. The very next time we gathered that same person Christopher B. Grimaldi, who we came to call Skip, arrived and heralded an intense and productive time for the development of the Moreton troop of scouts.

On troop nights we were encouraged to let off steam through 'wide games' usually in the Recreation ground woods or the area beyond or in our scout HQ with British Bulldogs. (I wonder if this is still a politically correct title). For the uninitiated this

I 'spect I grow'd

latter activity involves starting with everyone at one end of the hall with just one in the middle. Then on a given signal, everyone will rush to the other end attempting to avoid being caught. Those unfortunate to be waylaid then struggle to avoid being lifted off the ground to the cry of 'British Bulldog' by the captor(s). Those captured then join with the captors. The game continues with those still free running back and forth until everyone is in the middle bar maybe one or two. The game ends when all have been hoisted high with the last to be captured being declared the winner. At which point everyone will gather their dishevelled selves so as to look presentable for the more sedate closing ritual of the troop night.

About that time along came VE Day and VJ Day. The former proved to be quite momentous in various ways. At the time my mother was getting over a nervous breakdown, which meant that the two of us were living at my grandparents. On VE Day I cycled to Moreton only to find that my father was not at home but there was a message to say he had been involved in a car accident the previous day. He was returning from work at the Alvis plant near Stratford-upon-Avon in an MG Midget car driven by Ron Profitt when they collided with a lorry that was crossing the Fosseway at the Portabellow Cross Road near Shipston. My Dad was flung out and fortunately got away with only a few cuts and bruises but it was quite a shock to his system and to me as we thought we had got through the war without injury.

In the afternoon Skip turned up with an ambulance he had commandeered and loaded up a number of us to go swimming at Parson's Pleasure on the Cherwell at Oxford. This was a pleasant experience but alas I was a very weak swimmer then, which meant I could not get much pleasure from the activity. (Swimming facilities were very sparse at that time when the only pool available was an outdoor one privately owned at Broad Campden – now I am swimming 1500 metres every weekday before breakfast to keep fit).

In the evening of VE Day there was to be a firework display on the school field. I have presented this in the past tense as the fireworks that had been stored throughout the war period by Andrew Horne for such an occasion all caught fire soon after the start of the proceedings. For several minutes there was chaos with huge bangs and rockets whizzing and twisting horizontally in all directions. I vividly recall one snaking towards me and in my attempt to get out of the way ducked and promptly was hit on the side of the head – apart from a scorch mark I was OK. Quite an eventful day.

For VJ Day we had a celebratory Fete and sports event on the cricket ground, which was well attended and the weather was fine. One mischievous activity that a small group of us engaged in was to sneak under the canvas at the back end of the tent selling bottles of pop and take one away to share in the adjacent wood. However, it did not end there as after drinking the contents we refilled the bottle with urine, replaced the top and deposited it back in its original place in the tent. For the rest of the afternoon we hung around to see who would be the unfortunate person to buy it. Yes! It was one of our more distant associates. In our grubby and adolescent way we were all rolling around laughing at his misfortune – to this day this story has never been told and the recipient of the subterfuge is I guess still none the wiser who had committed such a felony.

Skip seemed to spend almost every spare moment with us in some way or other. He had a small grey Ford 8 car fitted with a cuckoo sounding device operated from a bellows inside and when this was operated it was similar to the effect of the Pied Piper on the rats of Hamelin – scouts appeared from nowhere. Regardless of whether or not it was a designated scout time we went off into the countryside learning and passing tests. The result of this kind of intensity was that many of us progressed at an extremely rapid rate through the various tests – second

I 'spect I grow'd

class, first class, bushman's thong, Kings Scout and at that time what were called all-round cords of various colours culminating in the treasured Gold Cord (later there were changes and the King's Scout became the top award). Clearly we were all into collecting proficiency badges of one kind or other. Two that particularly come to mind for me were the electrician and the pathfinder badges. To attain much of the skill associated with the former I visited and acquired knowledge and practice at the AWH workshop, a light engineering and electrical firm, which was situated on the corner of Wellington Road opposite the Public House. The helpful manager was George Long whom I had known from my Home Guard days.

For the pathfinder, badge we had to know something of the history of the town and be able to give clear directions to strangers on how to find various places. For the history we sat at the feet of a lovely man, the Reverend W.L. Warne (born 1862 and died February 1947) who had been a curate at both Broadwell and Moreton. I think it was three of us who sat and listened to his stories about Moreton history for several sessions. The one story that fired my teenage imagination was when he told us that before the building of the Redesdale Hall there would be bear baiting regularly on that spot. I am not sure about that story now as more recent scholarship has disputed some of his findings. However, he was a special person and much loved by everyone. After his death a *Short History of Moreton-in-Marsh* was edited and published by Kenneth Gil Smith of the Evesham Journal. I am informed that it has now become something of a collector's item.

A short while after Skip arrived we had another leader from the RAF Station. This was Flight Lieutenant Alan Winstanley DFC, an ex bomber pilot to become known to us all as Winnie, as a diminutive form of his family name. Winnie was a different but complementary addition to the leadership team. Whereas Skip was steeped in scouting practice Winnie was the entertainer. Before the War he had been in the Ralph Reader Gangshows and wore scarlet knee length socks with his scout uniform to prove it. Consequently with Winnie we were all singing *We're riding along on the crest of a wave and the sun is in the sky*, together with other gangshow numbers and acting out sketches. We also had our own version of *Much binding in the Marsh* with several verses about the troop written by Bill Beacham, one of our older members – we sang it to the tune that was used in the radio show.

In almost no time at all Moreton Scouts became what was the crack troop for Gloucestershire if not the country. For several years we sent all the King's Scout representatives from the county to the annual St Georges' Day parade before the King at the St George's Chapel Windsor. Being younger than some others I was later to gain this award and was probably one of the last to be privileged to attend this illustrious event. When eventually both Skip and Winnie left Moreton, Jack Strong, a local boy, who had returned from his War service, stepped in to look after the Troop. Jack had been a scout himself as a teenager and remained with Moreton Scouts for very many years serving in various capacities. However, an important aspect of scouting was to give service to the local community in some way and a number of us of us rose to the challenge. For example we spent several Saturdays cleaning the windows of Moreton Hospital. The task was rather like painting the Forth Bridge for there were and still are I imagine hundreds of small window panes needing attention. Fortunately we only worked on the windows at ground level but it was hard work, which led to a considerable feeling of satisfaction when completed. I remember the Matron being very grateful for our contribution.

Meanwhile back at school progress was steady. The one teacher I really admired was Ian Tilbrook the Geography teacher who had been a Major in the Marine Commandoes during WW 2 – so he was my kind of role model. Gradually, as I moved into the teenage years I became a typical stroppy adolescent, which had a profound effect on my academic progress as well as the kind of social life I wanted to lead. To some extent I became the class clown, which was a spirited action towards work avoidance.

I was brought to my senses when in class 4U we were told that if we did not do well in the French exam we would progress to 5R instead of 5U. Naturally I pulled out all the stops in the French exam and came fifth in class with 77%, which for the rest of my time was always referred to when I started to slack off again. Little did the teacher know that I was copying much of my French homework on the train coming to school usually from the two Doreens, namely, Doreen Harris (now Exton) and Doreen Hellier (now Guppy) – both well known personalities in Moreton. Philip Oliver Heatherley, or POH pronounced Po as a nickname, was a very effective teacher of French and constantly told us how good his results were. He also was a good teacher of what today would be called social education. In his lessons he would often provide us with anecdotes about life as well as lacing French conversation with personal references. For example I wore grey worsted flannel trousers, which were rather grand for school at that time. Consequently, he would tease me by reference to *Monsieur la Maison Blanche avec les pantalons magnifique.* It was a very skilled way of jollying along this recalcitrant adolescent for which I am now grateful. In order to give me some sense of responsibility in the fifth form and because I was one of the only people with a watch, I was made the bell monitor, which meant ringing the brass bell, located in the central area of the school, to mark the end of lessons. This provided me with a good excuse to wander round the school and if I was bored would often leave the classroom ten minutes before the ringing was due. However, this did not modify my behaviour and my school reports became steadily more appalling with comments such as *"Looks upon life as one huge joke"* and another *"Can we have less cheerful fooling and more cheerful work?"* I was often put outside the classroom door by some teachers who could not cope, which led me later as a teacher to never put anyone outside when I had to deal with difficult young people within the classroom setting and believe me I worked with some really difficult kids. When I look back I wonder how I ever reached the status I achieved in Education – perhaps it is something to do with the poacher becoming a gamekeeper.

With my infatuation for 'things' military and the scouts it was inevitable that I was keen on the School Corps. At fifteen it was the ATC with RAF blue uniform provided. However, it was decided that we could have Corps at fourteen, which meant that instead of ATC uniforms we were kitted out with ancient khaki uniforms acquired somehow I believe as rejects from Charterhouse School. These were extremely rough and uncomfortable with WW1 style puttees on our legs. We must have looked like refugees from the trenches but it was a uniform and we strutted around feeling like real men and ready for the next confrontation – well most of us felt like that but there were others who had misgivings about these quasi-military activities and in one or two cases refused to participate – I now realise how brave they were to resist the call. Captain Fitzhugh, a WW1 veteran, became Flying Officer for his role in the ATC, led us initially. He regaled us with stories of heroics from his army days and in the classroom threw blackboard rubbers at us if we were not paying attention. When he left, his position as the person in charge of the ATC was taken by three newcomers, namely Tom Fowles (maths teacher), Bill Howells (art teacher) and Albert Unstead (woodwork), who together developed the squadron along slightly more orthodox lines. Worthy of note is that the ATC squadron had a drum and bugle band, which led us on parades at certain times. This was a welcome diversion for some of us as on Corps afternoons those in the band would escape to the top of the field or the sports pavilion to practise out of earshot from the rest of the school.

In the midst of my secondary education came the winter of 1947, which is still considered to be one of the worst winters on record. In the Cotswolds we really suffered both from heavy snowfalls as well as plummeting temperatures. At the time we still had the RAF station functioning as a flying base with a meteorological station. This meant that weather reports were sent in frequently to the Air Ministry. The result of this was that Moreton-in-Marsh was national headline news on a number of occasions as the coldest place on record in the UK with minus 30 degrees plus of frost. However, it did not end there as the snow was very deep and often after snow falling overnight Moreton High Street was covered with around two to three feet of snow. This meant having to dig ourselves out, which culminated in a series of trenches crisscrossing the street to provide a network for movement. Clearly getting to school at Chipping Campden presented problems for many over several weeks. Most of the time the trains got through to Campden, which meant that we travelled and walked up the hill to school only to find, when we arrived, the Head had closed the school as those from the surrounding villages, both students and staff, could not get in. So we returned home and amused ourselves in the snow, often walking on the top of the hedgerows in the fields where the snow had drifted to be very deep indeed. How we kept warm in our homes with no central heating and heat from fires going up the chimney I do not know. It must have been very difficult for the elderly, but for those of us who were young it was all a big adventure.

I 'spect I grow'd

Scouting is largely about camping and expeditions of one kind or another. When I first joined, the tradition with Moreton Scouts was that the annual camp would be local, either at Hinchwick or at Cadley Clump. For those not familiar with the locality the latter is the prominent hill just beyond Batsford on the Aston Magna side. The first camp I attended was on the adjacent field looking down the hill towards Draycott. After a couple of days we were washed out as a result of having very old and leaky tents. Consequently we suffered for a while attempting to keep cheerful by singing *It ain't going to rain no more,* but in the end we returned home early. The next year was with Skip who familiarized us with much higher camping standards, which included cleaning the outside of the dixies and billycans with wire wool after each usage. This was the standard that we maintained along with scouring the site for litter daily with an inspection and points awarded. This was an anathema for all of us at first but soon we became very proud of the benchmark we had taken on especially when competing with other scout troops in the county.

For subsequent camps Skip was more ambitious and by then we had a parents' group that was intent on raising money for equipment and for expeditions further afield. We travelled to Conway in North Wales on two occasions and once to Otterton in Devon where we suffered from the incessant rain problem once again. For these camps we travelled on the bus owned by Ellis and Bull the only bus company in Moreton at that time. We also did our first sea crossing to Northern Ireland camping at Castledawson with a visit to Londonderry to experience the Orange Day marchers.

The really exciting and adventurous expedition was in 1948. This was with those who by then were termed senior scouts. Skip had left the RAF and Moreton but was still in touch. In his outrageous and imaginative way he decided that it was going to be a challenging and exciting activity where none of us would know our destination from one day to the next until we had arrived. Skip had conversations with all parents and reassured them that all would be well but did not disclose where we were heading. When the time came we set off in twos on bicycles with camping equipment and sealed instructions, which had to be opened after we had left. In fact each pair travelled by a different route camping overnight but all came together at Rugby School where we were met by one of the teachers who had been at Oxford (Keble College) with Skip. He showed us round the school and then took us to the railway station where we were put on an overnight train heading north. The guard was given our tickets, which meant that we did not know our destination until the following morning when were told by the guard to leave the train at Stirling in Scotland. We were met by a nurse called Marion who settled us in the local Scout HQ and then took us to see the Wallace Monument. Thereafter day-by-day we had new instructions that in turn took us on our bicycles and camping overnight or staying in Youth Hostels across the Trossacks, past Loch Lomond then to Fort William where we climbed Ben Nevis. Eventually we arrived on the Island of Tiree where Skip had been the Medical Officer at the small RAF Station there a few years earlier. Finally we found our way back to Fort William and caught the train for the homeward journey. For those who know David Day, formerly the reporter for the Evesham Journal in Moreton and district, this event was one of the first stories he reported on after taking up his post in 1948. He produced an update in the paper each week we were away, which made our journey an exciting and informative story for the readers.

For all these escapades you are asked to remember that this was only a short while after the end of WW2 when travel had not been the norm as it is for families and school children today. Therefore, for these country boys from Moreton-in-Marsh this was truly a big adventure and opened up our eyes to the British

I 'spect I grow'd

Isles preparing many of us for even greater escapades across the world in later years.

Alongside school and scouting a youth club opened, which was managed under the auspices of the YWCA with a fulltime Leader. Initially we had a purpose built club, which stood for many years in the grounds of the secondary modern school. After a couple of years in this building, for some reason unknown to me, another youth club building was erected at the entrance to the Landgate Fields. This was slightly larger than the original, which had now become part of the school. Perhaps the best known youth leader, who was influential for a number of years, was Winifred Everton (who settled down and married Peter Pritchard, a well known local photographer). Winifred organised a good number of interesting activities and was extremely hospitable. We did lots of dancing (ballroom and old time). I enjoyed especially dancing the quickstep to *Twelfth Street Rag* and always partnering for this number Ann Handy who was a good pal but never perceived as a *bona fide* girlfriend.

Winifred originated from Malvern and organised a trip to her home town during the festival where we saw a pageant on the life of Edward Elgar (now probably my favourite English composer along with music of the Austrian Gustav Mahler).

I am also reminded of the First Aid course leading to the award of a St. John's Ambulance Certificate, which enabled me to add the First Aider badge to my scout collection. Having competed that course, which was taken by a Doctor Struan-Marshall, from the RAF Medical Training Establishment (now set up at the RAF Station) we were offered a series on sexual matters. Around ten of us attended all the sessions, which were well presented with detail and for those times quite revolutionary. As a budding teacher I regaled some of my school friends with the received information on the school train the following day. When I look back I realise that this was probably the only reliable and informative help any of us received on personal relationships even if it was relayed second hand by yours truly.

Round about the time of my fourth or fifth year at the Grammar School the Pearman family, who lived at Fosseway House at the entrance to Fosseway Avenue, set up what was called the Fosseway Tennis Club. Mr and Mrs Pearman had three daughters Prudence, Rosemary and Christine (the latter now well known as Christine Dempster). Naturally we played a good deal of tennis but we also had many parties throughout the year all of which were most enjoyable and did much for our on-going social education. We were quite a select bunch, which included the young Ben Jeffrey as one of our number. What became a compulsory part of every party was that we all gathered on the lawn at midnight to dance that popular old-time 'square' dance called the Lancers to the music from *The Arcadians*. When I look back I realise how wise Mr and Mrs Pearman had been in bringing a group of young people together socially in their own home to give us plenty of freedom yet discreetly watching over us from a distance. I have some wonderful memories of those times and the people who were part of the group.

Another similar group that I joined during the winter months was a small Badminton Club that met in the Swan Room to the rear of the Public House. This may still be there. It was a little too short for a full size Badminton court, so the last couple of feet for the court the lines were actually painted upward on the end walls. This did not seem to deter our enjoyment of playing the game.

Some of us associated with these groups became younger associate members of the newly formed Moreton Hockey Club principally for women but also some mixed games. This was a game I latched on to as it was very close to the skills of cricket but subsequently also allowed me to wear spectacles in order to see the ball more clearly. In fact it became my main winter game both when I was in the RAF and as a student teacher of Physical Education at St. Pauls College, Cheltenham and Carnegie College, Leeds. Margery Strong who was a leading light in the development of the club employed a couple of us to mark the pitch out prior to the matches (played on the cricket ground) for which we were each rewarded with the princely sum of two shillings and sixpence for our efforts. I must confess that we were a bit slap happy about straight lines at times but teams seemed to manage OK.

A further way of earning a little pocket money resulted from my mother's friendship with the Harris family who farmed at Aston Magna. For a while I would go to the farm on Saturdays and clean out the pigsty and other areas for a few shillings. It was at this time that the Moreton Show was established and Stan Harris the farmer and a keen horseman became one of the prime movers in establishing the event, which was much more based on the idea of a Gymkhana than an agricultural show as it is at present. Knowing Stan I was given the opportunity to be one of the programme sellers, which was great fun moving around the showground and extracting half a crown from those who purchased a very glossy presentation. It also proved a 'nice little earner' as we were rewarded on the number of programmes we sold.

Soccer was the winter sport at school but I was rather too tall and gangly to ever be a moderately good player, so much so that I usually enjoyed being a goalkeeper rather than playing anywhere else. In later life I found that I gravitated more towards rugby football. In fact when appointed head of Physical Education at Alcester Grammar School (we used to play them when at CCGS) I got the job because the headmaster wanted to convert the school from soccer to rugby. However, as a teenager I followed the fortunes of Moreton Town Football Club watching and cheering at many of the home matches. Moreton has always been a strong footballing community and at that time had players such as Jim Allen in goal and later Alan

Stanley who took his place. Then there was Fred Hardiman and Billy Goddard, both semi-professional. Further on, my long-time friend Peter Lloyd played for the Town until he moved away.

An adolescent characteristic includes the desire to try out something new and different and for me at around the age of fifteen, still interested in wearing a uniform, I was attracted to the uniformed splendour of the Moreton Town Band. Alas I could not read music but I knew I was musical and they needed a side drummer so I went along. The conductor was a lovely man called Dan Hine, a postman during his working day, and around fifteen instrumentalists. Rehearsals were held in the youth club building on the school site. I am afraid I did not last long but time enough to don the uniform and march in the parade to the War Memorial for Remembrance Day. However, I found myself feeling guilty that I was not on parade with the Scouts and knowing where my true allegiance lay I left to focus on working towards my Kings Scout award.

At sixteen it was time to concentrate on gaining a school certificate, which I knew was essential if I wanted to fulfil my then goal of joining either the army or the RAF. However, there was a strong distraction to study, which was to be able to play cricket to a reasonable level. (photo – CCGS eleven) Cricket practice was held two or three evenings in the week during the season. A small group of us had some coaching from Andrew Horne, a prominent Moreton figure who had played for the Gloucestershire second eleven at some point. Surely, I could not miss this opportunity but what was the solution? It came to me that the sensible thing to do would be to go to cricket practice but to get up at the crack of dawn to complete homework and undertake revision. This worked out to be an ideal arrangement as at five o'clock in the morning I was much fresher and more alert than during the evening. Subsequently the exams came and went and I achieved a modest School Certificate. I was told by Mr. Heatherly when asked who would be returning for the sixth form that I would get just about enough to qualify but I could have gained a better result if I had really worked hard, which was at the time an anathema to me.

When I did enter the sixth form I chose to take Pure Maths, Applied Maths and Physics simply because all my mates were doing those subjects. Actually I should have taken French, Geography and History. My time as a sixth former was turbulent to say the least. About a month into studying I was involved in a fight with a fellow student called John Davenport (from Ilmington). We had moved up the school together and were actually very good friends. However, for some reason John got into the habit of taking a swing at the chin of everyone but just missing on purpose, which I found very irritating. As a result one day when he did this to me yet again I had to not miss but hit him fair and square on the chin, which resulted in a full blown fight in what was termed the Central Hall area just below the staffroom. The commotion we created disturbed Ian Tillbrook, who came down stairs, separated us and marched both of us off to Mr Bright the Headmaster. The head did not mince his words telling us that he was on the verge of creating new prefects and that neither of us would be appointed. Sadly this incident heralded the beginning of the end as far as my school career was concerned. I desperately wanted responsibility, which was now denied so matters went from bad to worse and at the end of one year in the sixth form I left under something of a cloud.

During this confused time at school an interesting opportunity arose back home at Moreton. The Redesdale Players, a local dramatic group had just been formed. The first production was to be *This Happy Breed* by Noel Coward and they wanted a young man to be the son Billy. I think it was David Day who approached me and asked if I was interested. Naturally being both an extrovert and a bit of a show off I leapt at the chance and enjoyed the experience and the esteem that came with the performance. Other members of the cast included David Day, Catherine Timms, Brenda Dee (now Gaden) Harold Everard, Mrs Tarplett and Mrs Beardsmore plus a young man from the RAF station. The producer / director was Mrs Smith-Maxwell from Lemington Grange. Joan Stapleton (mother of Guy) was the wardrobe and property person. It is interesting to note that later on Arnold Wesker, the well known playwright, who was undertaking his National Service at the RAF station became involved with the Redesdale players for a while. More about my association with Arnold Wesker (now Sir Arnold) in the next chapter.

Already I have mentioned the dancing and social life at school, which had now extended into the community life of Campden with regular dances being held in the Town Hall. Consequently this became an important venue for Saturday night hops.

I 'spect I grow'd

Around the time of being in the fifth and sixth form at school some of us, through developing friendships outside Moreton, became more involved with life at Chipping Campden. In the latter stages of this period I learnt to drive a car and was also the proud owner of a two-stroke motorbike, which enabled me to travel more extensively and with less physical effort.

For several years my friend Peter Lloyd and I attended the midnight Communion Service at Chipping Campden when after the service we would retire to the home of Roseanne Buckland in Park Road for refreshments. This always coincided with the return of the Campden Mummers who had been out regaling the town with the play during the evening and returned, each with quite a glow after the tipple being offered at each household on their round. Billy Buckland the leader of the Mummers was a real Cotswold character. He was from Romany gypsy stock and earned his living as a jobbing gardener. In fact the author Grahame Green, who lived in Campden for a while, mentions Billy in his autobiography as his gardener who, because of his gypsy origins, would eat snails that he had collected in the garden. Billy was also on Campden Town Council and his contributions to the discussions were often delivered with plain speaking in broad Gloucestershire dialect, which was charming and disarming but very much common sense. What he contributed is well reported and preserved in the pages of the *Evesham Journals* of that time

My first real girlfriend was Joan Horne, a year below me at school who had been the Campden May Queen (her Mother Phyllis was the music teacher at the Grammar School and father John was a stalwart of Campden society). The May Queen officiated at Scuttlebrook Wake, which later was combined with the reinstatement of the Cotswold 'Olympicks' on Dovers Hill. I attended this event whenever possible.

Photograph by Roland Dyer

It has now become a great social event especially with the torchlight procession and pipe band from the Hill to the Village at the end of the day.

And so at the age of seventeen and a half with schooldays at an end it was time to move on and blossom out into the big wide world. I was determined to join one of the forces and because of the combination of scouting and the Air Training Corps the Royal Air Force seemed to be the next step for me. Maybe with this modest background of both maths and physics plus a spirit of adventure I should attempt to become a pilot in the RAF, which moves me on beyond school days to life in the post school years and oddly enough brought me back to a different life and perspective of Moreton-in-Marsh.

I 'spect I grow'd

More photographs of Chipping Campden Grammar School

Upper Fifth 1949 with teacher Philip Heatherly

Upper Fifth 1950 with teacher Ian Tilbrook

Derrick Whitehouse

More photographs of Moreton Scout Troop in the 1940s

Camping at Conway, North Wales c.1947

Meal time at Conway

I 'spect I grow'd

Attending an event at Batsford 1945

Skip always led by example – Here he shows us how to clean dixies – inside and out

Derrick Whitehouse

Senior Scouts with hosts on Tiree 1948

Chapter five

The post-school years from 1950 to 1955

Upon leaving school it was a while before I could join either the RAF or the army as I was only seventeen. Consequently, I needed to earn some pocket money somehow for a few months. An offer came from our Group Scout Master Bill Dyer who on leaving the RAF at the end of WW2 had joined up with Arthur Lockyear to open a garage for the repair of cars and the sale of petrol in the London Road. For a limited period this seemed ideal as it provided me with an opportunity to learn more about how the motor car worked and acquire the ability to diagnose and treat minor faults plus a limited amount of driving. I also learnt how to swear as a result of having to tackle stubborn nuts and bolts that would not budge. Compared with contemporary garage facilities conditions were very primitive, especially for changing tyres when it was tyre leavers that had to be used and inner tubes had to be repaired in the old fashioned way with patches. I am afraid that in reality I came to understand that being a car mechanic was not the career I was seeking. Nevertheless at the time it was a pleasant interlude.

At around this time I had gained my King's Scout Award, which meant that two events were on offer. First there was the investiture and second the St George's Day parade at Windsor before the King and the rest of the Royal family. The investiture was held over a weekend in London aboard Captain Scott's ship the RRS Discovery. Naturally this was very special, meeting up with other King's Scouts from all over Britain. A number of visits to places of interest in London were arranged, which included Faraday House (the international telephone exchange) and the Ceremony of the Keys at the Tower of London. On the Sunday morning we attended a service at St Martin in the Fields.

A short period later was the parade at Windsor, which was very moving, being led by a military band around the quadrangle before the King (who looked very frail), the Queen and the princesses. For me the highlight was the service in St George's Chapel and I often remark that one of my early spiritual experiences was that of being one of a thousand or so male voices singing in unison the hymn *For all the saints....*

The time came to see if I could become a pilot in the RAF. In those days this involved around five days for selection at the

I 'spect I grow'd

RAF station at Hornchurch in Essex. Each day we encountered a variety of aptitude tests and interviews. With National Service still compulsory there were very many of us up for selection. With my background with the ATC proficiency behind me, which included the theory of flight along with aspects of navigation plus my maths and physics I felt comfortable with the tests. However, when it came to the results around half a dozen of us had our names called separately and taken off to a room where we were confronted individually by a Medical Officer and one other. I was told that although I had passed the aptitude test for aircrew I was found permanently medically unfit for flying duties due to the deterioration in my eyesight. Consequently, that was the end of that ambition, which meant turning to plan B.

Compared with today, in those times there was little guidance given to help individuals to make wise decisions and as I look back on my life I can only believe that at best there was some form of divine intervention on how my life worked out. By then I was aged around seventeen and nine months, which meant that from seventeen and a half it was possible to volunteer for a service of one's choice rather than wait for call up and be directed. There was also a second advantage in terms of pay. For a two year national service conscript initial pay was 27 shillings a week. By volunteering for either three or five years the starting pay was £3 and 3 shillings. I went for the five year option and a couple of weeks before my eighteenth birthday in November arrived for kitting out at RAF Cardington in Bedfordshire. For that week it was all very friendly and cosy, then we moved to RAF West Kirby on the Wirral where everything changed. Every ex-serviceman or woman will have tales to tell about their own square bashing experience. (Arnold Wesker recorded the experience in his play *Chips with Everything*). Actually it was tough but I loved almost every minute because I was good at everything. In fact I was so accomplished that at the end of the eight weeks and the passing out parade I was selected for the task of being the parade marker, which entailed marching alone across the parade ground to a spot upon which the thousand or more recruits had to fall in. A proud moment for somebody who fancied his chances as a potential commissioned officer in the RAF Regiment. Except that this was not going to be the way forward.

We all had to have a trade interview to work out the next step in our career. I set out my desire to be commissioned in the Regiment only to be told that at that time there were no vacancies due to all posts being taken up by wartime officers who had decided to stay on. Often these were so called redundant aircrew. So did I want to go into the Regiment as a gunner which was a different scenario altogether? The answer was an emphatic No!

Where to then, as I was now in for five years and had to make the best of it? The answer I came up with was that I wanted to work with people and had acquired a developing interest in Psychology. It seemed that the best trade for this pursuit could be the medical branch of the RAF. Now where was the Medical Training Establishment? Why of course it was at RAF Moreton-in-Marsh.

Scout brothers in arms – Brian Davies (Navy) Derrick W (RAF) Peter Lloyd (RAMC)

On completion of the basic training and a spot of leave I arrived at RAF Moreton towards the end of January 1951. Several of us had to wait for a new course to start and were put into a holding flight, which meant that we spent some time doing fatigues of one kind and another around the site but we had a certain amount of freedom and spare time. The weather was very cold and some snow about. One day a rumour went round the camp that there was no coal or coke available and that the establishment was to close down for a week or two. On this particular day at lunch time I decided to go into Moreton on my motor bike and as was my habit called in to see David Day in the office of the Evesham Journal and innocently I told him about the pending closure of the RAF station. Unbeknown to me at the time David saw this as a good story and an opportunity for lineage at a national level what with the Cold War and the nation being on alert. Surely this could be a chance for the Russians to do something spectacular if other bases followed suit. The next day the national papers were full of the story and the RAF decided that closing was no longer an option. Coal had to be brought in from somewhere. That somewhere turned out to be from Wythall near Birmingham where an RAF station had closed down. To get the coal, lorries had to go out from Moreton with airmen on board to shovel the coal and return to unload at the base. There was just the ready-made group to undertake this task, namely, the holding flight with yours truly as a member. For four or five days we toiled, shifting many tons of coal and coke to save the day. I certainly never let on to the rest of the group that I was the one who had caused this turn of events, which was a great lesson to me about being more discreet with classified information. However, David is still one of my best and longest lasting friends claiming that this was the best scoop of his career in journalism.

For the two months of the basic training course to become a Nursing Attendant I had to live in a billet on the RAF station. However it was possible to get home and to participate in weekend activities. One such event was a dance held in Moreton Town Hall to select a Festival Queen for the Festival of Britain celebrations later in the year. When it came to the time to choose Miss Moreton-in-Marsh as well as having a few local beauties, a very attractive young WRAF woman was persuaded to come forward for possible selection. I am afraid I cannot recall just how this was accomplished but the WRAF contender won the day. It is possible to understand what murmurings took place within the Moreton community that a native girl had not been chosen. When I reflect on this issue I tend to feel it was a very sensible PR stunt on the part of Moreton to integrate the RAF into a closer friendship with the native community.

As far as the course was concerned the whole lot was very new to my experience. I found everything interesting but decided that being a male nurse was not to be my vocation. Consequently when they were recruiting for people to train as dispensers I presented myself and was selected to join the six month course, which would be starting a few months after the completion of my basic training. For this interim period I was posted to work in the Station Sick Quarters at RAF Lyneham but returned to Moreton as a Leading Aircraftsman when the course started.

The dispenser programme was very informative and I launched into it with considerable optimism. Another plus was that I was allowed to live at home and participate in the community life of the Cotswolds. Often I would have lunch in the NAAFI and it was here that I encountered Arnold Wesker. The trainee dispensers were quite a bright bunch and sitting together we were seen by Arnold (known to us as Wizzy) as an interesting group to be with. One member of our group was particularly intelligent and engaging. She was Corporal Enid Franklin who had been to public school and had a very engaging and up-market voice. Wizzy called her *Duchess*. Arnold was not impressed with National Service with the result that his trade was that of an *Admin Orderly*, which for those who do not know this term means to be a general dogsbody who could be used anywhere to undertake menial but essential tasks. Arnold worked on the dustcart collecting rubbish, which made no demands on his intellect and provided him with a reasonable amount of spare time. He used this time to write poetry and we were privileged to be regaled by his latest composition during our lunch period when sometimes he would actually stand on the table to deliver to the assembled company.

Around this time I also learned about the holy of holies on the camp. In other words in the Station Headquarters building there was a room known as Bomber Harris's Room, which presumably had been used by the Air Marshal at some point. Whether he planned the thousand bomber raids from this room is a matter for conjecture. In fact it may simply be part of the mythology that was circulating in the RAF.

Very soon after the start of the course the Medical Training Establishment was moved from Moreton to Freckleton / Lytham in Lancashire. It was there that I realised that I did not wish to be shut in to work in a dispensary day after day and I applied to be released not only from the course but also from training. This was granted and I applied to join the Junior Administration course, which would take me rapidly to the substantive rank of Corporal and onward to be a Sergeant in Medical Administration.

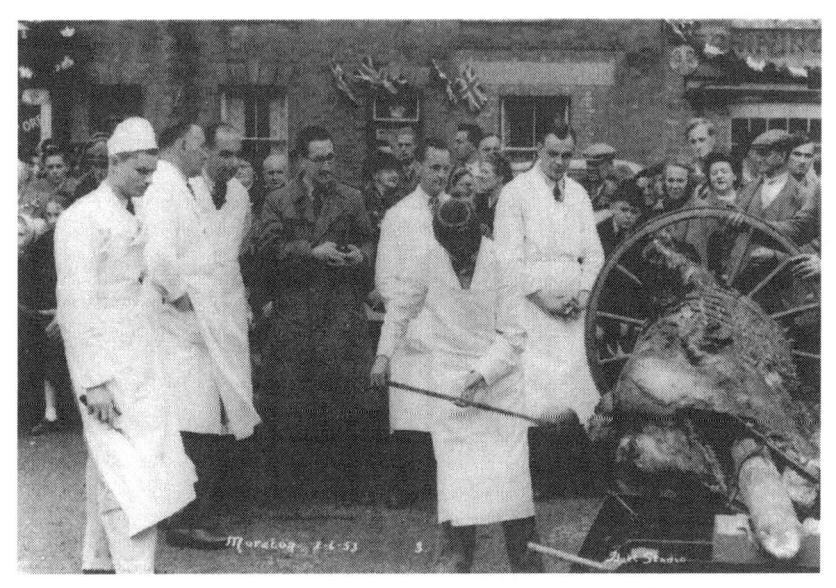

Ox Roast – Coronation Day 1953

After a short spell in charge of the Station Sick Quarters at RAF Westwood at Peterborough it was time for the Coronation of Queen Elizabeth in 1953. I was at home for this event on embarkation leave and watched the proceedings on the TV owned by Mr and Mrs Percy Lloyd who had shops at 3 Oxford Street.

Within around ten days I was on a troopship the *Empire Trooper* with all the Commonwealth forces who had attended the Coronation heading for Ceylon (now Sri Lanka) where I spent the next two and a half years and the end of my time in the RAF. What happened whilst in Ceylon is another story and not appropriate for this volume. However, it needs to be suggested that it was this experience that included dealing with many of the wounded being repatriated by air from the Korean War that had a profound influence on my later becoming a pacifist and a Quaker.

I returned to the UK in October 1955 where I was demobilised at RAF Innsworth near Gloucester. Not quite knowing what to do in Civvy Street I consulted an employment agency for ex-service personnel in Cheltenham where I was encouraged to train as a school teacher at St. Pauls College in Cheltenham. The fortunate thing about being trained at St Pauls as a teacher is that it was an all male college and because the majority had experienced the world through National Service we were treated like adult males rather than people who had just left school. This was particularly made manifest in the compulsory course we all were called to undertake and known by the old fashioned term Divinity. The course content was geared up to men of the world by introducing us to a wide range of adult topics, which related very much to the trials and tribulations of every-day life. The two year course had already started but I was accepted on condition I undertook a teaching practice during college Christmas vacation period. The obvious place to undertake this task was at the Secondary Modern School at Moreton-in-Marsh where the Headteacher was Mr A.L. Lock. This proved a reassuring experience as up to then I was not sure that working in education was the right direction for me to take. In fact it was and I had a wide-ranging experience and rewarding life in teaching, teacher training and administration.

Naturally whilst at St.Paul's I was able to get over to Moreton quite often and easily. One such time was during the dispute over the *Duck Pond*. For those not familiar with the issue it revolved round half the pond being owned by one person and the other half by another agency where one of the owners had a desire to fill in the half owned by them, which would block the flow of water as well as make the pond too small. The whole town was in uproar and loyalties and opinions were divided. The only solution was to have a public meeting to try and resolve the matter in the Town Hall. The night for the meeting came and the place was packed with a large percentage of the population. Feelings ran high and I recall two incidents during the evening. A local doctor rose to his feet to speak only to be shouted down by Stan Hathaway a local character and birthright Moretonion with "Sit down mister you an't bin here five minutes" to the amusement of most of the assembly. The second happening was when at the height of the debate, ducks were released to fly all around the hall. These had been smuggled in by John Rolph and his wife who farmed at Todenham but John was a native of Moreton. In the end the matter was rested and ultimately led to the cleaning and upkeep of what at the time was something of an eyesore. Now it is an endearing feature assisting Moreton to maintain something of a pleasing rural ambiance.

From St. Pauls I moved on into the world of education. To progress meant that I changed jobs regularly. Moreton was always where my parents were and from 1963 my mother was on her own. We constantly visited Moreton with my family and for very many years my mother saved the *Evesham Journal* for me to read so that I could keep up to date with life in my beloved Cotswolds. Even now when my mother is no longer with us I cannot resist undertaking a regular visit and carrying out a tour of inspection to see what changes have taken place and if anyone wants to listen while I regale them with stories of growing up in Moreton during the 1930s and 1940s.

Epilogue

As Time Goes By!
The continuing story of nostalgia and questing into the 21st century

We all have memories good or not so good of the place where we spent our formative years and hopefully we feel that we have been very fortunate in our upbringing as a result of communicating with the people we met during that period.

Later in life we have flashbacks with, as we do get older, feelings of nostalgia, not to return to the past but maybe a realisation of the powerful influence those early days have had on the way life has unfolded. Also when you visit places from the past it is possible to commune with ghosts from that period either people or even the buildings.

Frequently when I visit the Cotswolds and especially Moreton and Chipping Campden I walk around and cannot help but recall those who lived in certain houses or the activities we undertook together in particular buildings but above all the people we encountered. Sometimes I have been known to walk around the cemetery at Moreton looking at the gravestones to remind me not only of the locals but also the RAF personnel who lost their lives during the Second World War.

What has been written in this volume represents just the tip of the iceberg in terms of what my early life was really all about and certainly in words it is impossible to project the feelings of the times. Photographs can help but it is probably the feelings that I recall when I visit rather than the detail of the experiences that are vital in reminiscing.

I have mentioned many names and there will be those still around that I grew up with who will be able to have similar visions and feelings about certain individuals whom I have referred to. How can I convey to the more recent inhabitants the vision I still have of some of the characters that have been described?

In a paradoxical way my life away from Moreton has served to make my recollections even more vivid and in perspective. I have not only lived and worked in many interesting parts of the UK – such as Warwickshire, Soham in Cambridgeshire, the Cities of Bath and Liverpool but have travelled to many parts of the world as well. In addition I have been fortunate to gain experience and qualifications in Physical Education, Religious Education, Guidance and Counselling along with attaining a Masters Degree and a PhD in education, faith and moral development and the social sciences. Collectively these experiences have enabled me to look objectively at my childhood and teenage experience in a way where I can understand and appreciate the process that has made me who I am today.

The conclusion I come to is that I was so very fortunate to be born and live through a time when life was fairly tough yet was embraced by a loving and caring community. By community I mean there was stability from the local population but life was enhanced by a frequently changing populace that brings a vibrant and fresh countenance to a small market town that may have slipped into the doldrums without the injection of passing but ephemeral residents. Perhaps that is how Moreton has always been since the Romans were passing through on the Fosseway or the drovers and other travellers stopping over at the crossroads in one or other of the local coaching inns. All

I 'spect I grow'd

this brought trade and prosperity as well as enlightenment to the indigenous population.

So what does all this mean and how does it impart on who I am now? Because of my background in education I cannot help but align my experience as a child with what is now perceived as spiritual development. I believe life is a spiritual (not necessarily religious) quest for everyone. It is important to emphasise that spirituality in my understanding does not necessarily mean allegiance to a particular faith or even belief system. When considering the conditions where spiritual growth will flourish I turn to David Hay and Rebecca Nye for guidance from their book called *The Spirit of the Child*. They outline three forms of sensing that need to be present and inter-related within our lives and the surrounding culture if spirituality is to be truly nurtured, which are:

- Awareness sensing – where one focuses on the here and now and is able to tune in to particular experiences whilst in the flow so as to focus on all the senses be they pleasant or disagreeable.

- Mystery sensing – is concerned with our imagination setting us out to explore the mysteries of life and develop a sense of awe and wonder and oneness with the universe.

- Value sensing – where we experience the delights and despair of daily life to sense ultimate goodness along with meaning and understanding of human nature and all creation.

To illustrate what this means to me I turn to an experience I had many years ago when I was involved in teacher education in Liverpool. I was supervising a student in an inner-city primary school where there were no trees or even a blade of grass to be seen anywhere. Whilst in conversation with the class teacher he told me that a couple of weeks earlier he had taken his class to a field study centre in North Wales for a few days. The first morning he was out with his class looking around when a boy came running up to him and said "Eh Sir – I didn't know there were so many greens!" I cannot think of a better example that embraces all three forms of sensing. What happened could have been the lad's initial moment of spiritual knowing. I maintain that throughout our lives, whether we are aware of it or not, there are opportunities for this type of spiritual sensing being generated and nowhere is it felt more than at the heart of growing up and our experience of community life in all its forms.

Unlike the lad in Liverpool I was surrounded by all the greens and the beauty of the Cotswold countryside and probably simply perceived this as the norm. This along with a loving family and a plethora of friends provided me with security, which allowed me to explore values through both the rewarding as well as more harsh experiences. Clearly the experience afforded through the muscular Christianity of being a boy scout had a profound effect not only at the time but has stayed with me throughout my life. Then the sense of mystery evolved through a whole range of experiences as an inquisitive and sometimes questioning young person. I now realise that a sense of awe and wonder can be released during moments of discovering things that to an adult seem quite mundane. For example the day we each discover that two plus two makes four. However, this notion can be applied to almost any learning situation.

From this base of spiritual learning many of us develop a feeling that there is something there that is beyond the self. The seeds of this kind of knowing were clearly sown during my early life and I have been fortunate to have interacted with people who have assisted in my developing a more mature and enlightened perception of what all this can mean.

Faith means *The assurance of things hoped for; a conviction of things not seen* (Paul's letter to the Hebrews). Putting faith in these terms suggests to me that everyone can have faith even if they have trouble with God. Growing up as I did with no pressure at all over alignment with a particular church – I never once went to a Sunday School, presented me with a broad outlook on life generally and I have always been seen as a maverick professionally, which may have been initiated by my bolshie non-conformist teenage years.

Perhaps the best that I can expect out of life and the influence of my formative years can be summarised by the title of the second book by Barack Obama, which was the theme of the sermon delivered on his first time of worship in a Christian Church, namely – *The Audacity of Hope* – I feel that this encapsulates what was the design for my childhood and teenage years growing up in the Cotswolds all those years ago during the 1930s and 1940s, which spills over to the audacious person I now am at the beginning of the twenty first century in my late seventies.

'Do you know who made you?' 'Nobody, as I knows on,' said the child ... I 'spect I grow'd. Don't think nobody made me.'

From *Uncle Tom's Cabin* Chapter 20. (The child is Topsy)

Printed in Great Britain
by Amazon